T0304967

The 0.1% Academy

The 0.1% Academy

*Master the 7 Mindsets to Maintain
Peak Performance*

GARETH TIMMINS

First published by Nicholas Brealey Publishing in 2024
(from September 2024 known as John Murray Business)
An imprint of John Murray Press

1

A CIP catalogue record for this title is available from the British Library

Hardback ISBN 978-1-39981-4-850
UK ebook ISBN 978-1-39981-4-881
US ebook ISBN 978-1-39981-5-512

Typeset by KnowledgeWorks Global Ltd.

Printed and bound in Great Britain by Clays Ltd, Elcograf S.p.A.

John Murray Press policy is to use papers that are natural, renewable and recyclable
products and made from wood grown in sustainable forests. The logging and
manufacturing processes are expected to conform to the environmental
regulations of the country of origin.

John Murray Press   John Murray Business
Carmelite House   123 S. Broad St., Ste 2750
50 Victoria Embankment   Philadelphia, PA 19109
London EC4Y 0DZ

John Murray Press, part of Hodder & Stoughton Limited
An Hachette UK company

The sharp edge of performance is produced via an often beautiful interplay and entanglement of both mental and physical exertion. Whereas a conditioned mind can carry the body through fatigue and injury, when the mind falls out of sync with the demands of the body and the environment – due to a lack of self-awareness, monitoring and mitigation – you can forget about your wellbeing, the maintenance of performance and thus your pursuit of success.

Gareth Timmins

Contents

Introduction

In early 2013, I was in the midst of a frightening and uncontrollable mental health disorder. While waiting to deploy to Afghanistan, as a hostile environment Close Protection Operator, I felt anything but the elite soldier and public perception of a Royal Marines Commando. As a result of cognitive burnout – fuelled by a history of obsessive compulsive disorder (OCD) – I was experiencing vivid and disturbing intrusive thoughts, an unrelenting torment that shattered my sense of who I was and made my perceived identity a fraud.

Ten years of pushing myself relentlessly to achieve and assure prosperity by 'applying resilience' had now created a monster of mental debilitation. Seven years after leaving Commando Training Centre Royal Marines (CTCRM) successfully, I suddenly found myself a shadow of my former self. What was once a finely tuned mindset was now creating depictions of my death and mortality at will, without warning and in the most bizarre ways conceivable.

How on earth did it come to this? After everything: all the training, the personal investment and a lifetime's exposure to elite environments that demanded resilience and the very best performance outcomes. How did I arrive here in such a dark, frightening and fragile mental state? More to the point, could it have been avoided?

Three years ago, when I mapped out the seven phases in this book, I did so because I felt I could have done things better to cushion my own fall into burnout. At the end of a long day, we are only human, confined by an organic, fragile body and a cognitive processing system that is subconsciously aware of this fragility. By understanding that the application of indefinite resilience and sustained focus is fraught with unacknowledged limitations, and thus unforeseen dangers, we can arm ourselves with the tools needed to maximise performance while safeguarding our mental health.

This book documents a handful of life experiences and important lessons I have learned since leaving CTCRM and my journey to discover what it takes to maintain peak performance at an elite level. How our state of mind is not a constant but rather a fluid cycle of seven mindsets. A process of self-regulation that, once understood and managed, means you can reach the peak of performance and stay there, or recover quicker from burnout and regain high-performing behavioural alignment to remain on course.

The 0.1% Academy is a place where you will discover how to build a relentless pursuit and thirst for growth and achievement while exploring, via psychological lessons and analysis, the cognitive impact sustained when faced with challenges. As we do so, I will share my personal experiences of moments of stark realisation, career disillusionment, life-changing transitions and the emergence of mental illness through a lack of effective mitigation.

I will share research and applications for establishing cognitive stability when performing at an elite level in any sport or profession, and explore how to perform better for longer while upholding our mental wellbeing. We will learn that success itself can be ugly and often leave battle scars, but that a continuous journey to goal fulfilment, working through the success mindset cycle, can be perpetually rewarding.

I did very badly at school. I could not read fluently until I was in my teens and even then I found it incredibly difficult to stand up in class and read a paragraph or a page out loud. Two things were at play. First, I could neither concentrate nor keep still, and every single parents' evening and school report concluded with: 'Gareth is easily distracted.' Second, I was totally focused on rugby being my future career and on becoming a professional player. These two things combined to sabotage my education and left me wondering whether I was intelligent or not.

When I reached my twenties, I was often credited with being switched on and somehow different from others. I picked things up very quickly without the need for additional support or training. I enjoyed deep conversations and was always trying to work out ways in which we could improve ourselves from a human performance perspective. I was also very keen on my personal development. While my colleagues in the Marines or in private security would sit and watch movies, I took courses and read about businesses or how to make money.

At around the age of twenty-eight, I decided to see if I could cut it academically. I had already completed the hardest physical (and arguably mental) course in the world and I wanted to explore whether I could complete one of the hardest academic courses in the world, so I embarked on Forensic Psychology. In an attempt to innovate, I wanted to merge security risk management with forensic psychology; to focus more on human behaviour and the social issues or psychological mechanisms that promoted criminal or terrorist activities.

Going to university gave me the opportunity to investigate my thoughts and ideas and then articulate them through my writing, as well as equipping me with a fundamental understanding of psychology, social science and the construct of human behaviour. However, there did not seem to be much appetite to explore new approaches in the field of security and forensic psychology. Although I was eternally grateful for the academic journey, I began to feel that it was not a fully worthwhile professional venture.

In 2015, I worked as head of global security for a venture capital start-up in Mayfair, London. I became very close to the CEO and he learned of my interest in creativity and entrepreneurialism. As a result, for Christmas he bought me tickets to attend the 'Unleash the Power Within' convention headed up by Tony Robbins at the ExCel exhibition centre, in London.

While the experience was intensive and in some parts quite extreme, Tony said one thing during the weekend that sparked a chain reaction in me:

> Everyone in this room has at least one thing they know they should be doing; one thing that if they committed to it and saw it through, would positively change the course of their lives … I want you to write down what that is and if you do, you must commit to seeing it through [and] making it come to fruition!

I wrote down: 'Write up the diary entries and bring the book to life.' This would later be published as my first book, *Becoming the 0.1%*. That title referred to probably the best Royal Marines advert ever: '99.9% Need Not Apply'. This was an actual statistic in 2003, representing the odds of success from walking into a recruiting office to reaching the end of training and getting a coveted Green Beret. Only 0.1% (1/1000) made it through the process from start to finish. It is also the mindset under the microscope and behind this second book, *The 0.1% Academy*.

When I look back now, it is obvious that university came at a pivotal moment in my life. Upon meeting my literary agent in early 2020, I had just completed my studies when he challenged me to include a lesson for the reader at the end of each chapter, one that they could use to nourish their lives. I was only able to extract the teachings within each week of the diary due to the unbelievable coincidence of studying psychology and gaining a rich understanding of human behaviour, but also gaining the ability to impart that knowledge with the pen and merge it with my own experience to share what I had learned.

My ultimate aim in *The 0.1% Academy* is to dispel our socially constructed understanding about elite or growth mindsets and equip you with the awareness, understanding and skills to find and maintain your own successful outcomes for longer. We will do this by exploring the pitfalls to avoid and then by working through a practical programme of steps to configure your optimum success mindset cycle.

From early childhood and throughout our lives, many of us will strive constantly to improve ourselves – to dismantle or refine the person we are and will become. Despite educational status, there is a sense of general understanding known as folk psychology that a certain 'mindset' or outlook on life is not only responsible for success but essential if someone is to reach their goals.

For me, developing an elite mindset that delivers success requires the interplay of two qualities: the innate, inherited genetically from our parents and ancestors, along with the culture(s) and experiences we are exposed to during our lifetime. In recent years, 'mindset' has become a hot topic, with many people wanting to understand and apply these qualities to enhance their lives. The qualities under the microscope are usually those that produce the extraordinary – whether that is through the resilient military mindset, learning from the behavioural habits of elite sporting professionals, or gaining insights and lifestyle coaching from high-achieving business CEOs or world-renowned innovators.

Performing at your optimum level, whether mental, physical or an intertwining of both, is an outcome that captures the imagination of everyone, regardless of their sporting background, intelligence or appetite for physical exertion. If someone is manipulating the mind to produce truly remarkable results or physical capabilities, we are intrigued to know how they achieved it so that we might do the same.

However, while chasing down the idyllic, elite mindset that underpins such outcomes, we fail to acknowledge and appreciate its limitations. A reality that no matter where we fall on the mindset spectrum, once it has been acquired and calibrated to achieve the desired outcome, it is never stable or robust enough to assure repeated and unimpeded success. It requires constant maintenance, investment and the 'manipulation' of self-regulation to remain finely tuned.

In many ways, the safeguarding of our minds is no different from the intricate care and strategy given to a Formula One car during a Grand Prix race. Despite the perceived embodiment of resilience in elite mindsets from folk psychology, I believe that mindset is constantly in transit and often elusive, therefore mental health issues are never too far away.

This book uncovers the fluidity of elite mindsets by looking at seven stages through a personal dissection of the 'growth mindset', exploring one overarching goal or repeated success cycle. In doing so, this book hopes to dispel the popular culture's perspective surrounding the perceived resilience and plasticity of such mental states. It explores the internal conflict that is created for some individuals by exposure to highly competitive, high-stake occupations and environments, and highlights how this can result in mental fatigue and even mental illness if management is neglected.

In 2020, I founded Nought Point One, an emerging functional fitness clothing brand and performance hub, focusing on disciplines such as CrossFit, Hyrox and other extreme sports, inspired by the operational requirements of the Royal Marines. The brand specialises in distinctive activewear as well as self-help and smart-thinking publications, along with mindset coaching and training programming for the military, high-intensity competitions and running events.

As I look forward, I have started preparing the premise for Book Three, while exploring PhD research with the University of Surrey. The topic under investigation is how to 'Gauge Atmospherics' in our environment. In particular, how hostile environments and high-threat social encounters influence our psychology and initial behavioural response, informing instant and effective decision-making via the removal of 'top-down' bias to ensure survival during hostile or life-threatening situations.

Through the usage and lens of Augmented Reality (AR), we plan to simulate hostile situations in controlled settings to see if we can elicit such phenomena within corporate environments, to facilitate better decision-making practices and thus contribute to corporate innovation.

Nought Point One is quite literally an organic manifestation of being on this journey of self-help and performance, working with key organisations such as KIA Motors, Caterpillar, National Highways, Leeds Rhinos, Doncaster College and the University of Surrey. In addition, Nought Point One supports elite human endeavours striving to make a difference to the planet and its inhabitants.

Gareth Timmins, 2024

CHAPTER ONE

The Misconception of Elite Mindsets

Since leaving the Royal Marines in 2011, I have found the perceived identity difficult, if not impossible, to shift. Upon completing training and during my time in the Royal Marines, I revelled in the public's impression of this Marine identity: often deemed fearless, with an ability to kill at will utilising all manner of objects and, bizarrely, to manipulate anyone to the point of death with our bare hands. The reality could not be further from the truth.

The fact is that completing Royal Marines training equips you with an unbelievable mindset, which is underpinned by self-confidence. That is incredibly powerful. As a by-product, you also get a truly mind-blowing level of fitness. Upon finishing training, Royal Marines recruits are said to possess fitness levels within the top 1 per cent in the world, in the same category as elite Olympic athletes. Yes, we receive intensive training to execute the role requirements and responsibilities, but we do not leave Commando Training Centre as experts in unarmed combat. In fact, the Hollywood depictions of hand-to-hand combat are a fraud.

Arguably, such misplaced presumptions of identity serve a young Marine well during their more youthful years within society. However, for me, with maturity and ever-changing life circumstances, there came an eventual decision to leave the Royal Marines, which sparked a tricky period of transition back into society. At this stage, the concept of this Marine identity – the ruthless, mindless killer – became a hugely damaging and frustrating disadvantage to my successful reintegration into civilian life.

Frustratingly, although I left the Royal Marines some thirteen years ago, people still place that occupation front and centre when analysing me. In nearly all my social encounters or within the workplace, despite having done other occupations for much longer, that Marine identity remains rigid in people's minds. It has consistently overshadowed nearly all my subsequent life endeavours – often detrimentally – to potential employers. People naturally assume I will not be fazed by any physical conflict and that in some way I am emotionless and thus unempathetic.

Ultimately, people arrive at one conclusion: 'He's intimidating.' Such words are not uttered, but I know that those alarm bells have sounded subconsciously. This is the result of a perception of military personnel being robotic – the belief that they cannot operate and think independently without following orders – leading to the ultimate evaluation that I am therefore 'not the correct fit for corporate environments'.

A few years ago, I worked for a digital NHS provider and encountered two biased presumptions. First, when I displayed empathy for others, it was immediately commented on. I was told, 'I'm quite shocked how empathetic you are towards others and how well you adapt and thrive in different social situations and encounters.'

Another one came when I was dismissed by the organisation for reasons out of my direct control. During a debrief, I was informed of the reasons for dismissal. While responding to the claims, I was met with this comment: 'I am sure a man with your background and given what you have experienced won't be fazed or affected by this decision given what you must have been through in your life to date … therefore, I don't feel that bad delivering this news.'

Although it was grossly inaccurate to assume such a thing, the comments were grounded in stereotypical arrogance: a false belief insinuating that I lacked intellect or emotional bearing and had become desensitised to what was deemed a non-life-threatening situation. A misjudgement we often attach to people who undertake taboo or extraordinary occupations.

The truth is, I once believed the same misrepresentation.

I joined the Royal Marines when I was twenty years old. Until that point, I believed mindset was fixed once a particular pre-scription of thinking was achieved through experience – you could argue this is a universal inference. For example, I whole-heartedly assumed upon reaching the end of training and becoming a Royal Marines Commando that I would become so mentally resilient that I could deal with all of life's chal-lenges without becoming stressed and showing emotion. But more so, that this prescription of thinking would endure.

Much of my early misunderstanding about the rigidity of mindset derived from a common portrayal embodied in nearly all 1980s' and 1990s' action war films. For example, *Rambo*, starring Sylvester Stallone, where the main character is seem-ingly unfazed and unemotional to the point of vacancy when confronted with all types of war, conflict and the often drasti-cally unequal survival dynamics. Naively, I figured this fictional depiction of mindset to be attainable – a crucial factor I deemed to be an absolute necessity if I was to achieve my future life ambitions. That was why I aspired to join the Royal Marines.

However, throughout the subsequent ten months of elite military training, I arrived at an uncomfortable realisation: my emotions could not simply be turned off. Despite all the arduous training, they required consistent regulation. I still had to control my personal anxieties and manage my fears – two emotions at the latter stages of training that I had presumed would naturally become vacant.

That said, the intensive course requirements demanded that recruits learn how to manage their emotional responses in order to navigate their way successfully through the often crippling adversity posed by training, while bearing the daily burden of the fear of failure.

Unknowingly, this process was building what I call 'intrinsic self-confidence' – the type that forms when you finally back yourself to get out of a tough situational exposure and to do so with consistency, without the need for external encouragement. The by-product of which is the self-assuring knowledge one is handed by experience that allows the recruits to trust themselves implicitly, to overcome any obstacle or challenge that stands before them. For me, that is the key to success.

While the emotional alert bells still sounded for all of us towards the end of Commando Training, the remaining recruits embodied a sense of comfort in the self, knowing that they had the mental tools to succeed despite fatigue, injury and overwhelming adversity. Quite frankly, we had become temporarily desensitised to withstand the cognitive pain and through a process of mental conditioning, we were able to endure the repetitive suffering elicited by that raw and brutal exposure.

Nonetheless, to my astonishment, by the end of the course I was not Rambo – vacant and unemotional. I was human, still wrestling with my emotions like anyone else, while trying desperately to achieve composure in order to complete the infamous Commando Tests.

Faulty misconceptions about mindset are not confined solely to the military. We are often guilty of the same misjudgements when it comes to sporting athletes, or those in any other profession that demands an extraordinary mental resilience.

For example, Simone Biles, arguably the greatest female gymnast of all time, dramatically withdrew during the 2020 Tokyo Olympics due to a 'mental block'. She stated that this was due to the 'twisties', a frightening state of dissociation between body position and the ground, elicited by a feeling of being lost in the air.

Despite Simone's sudden lack of confidence and the anxiety that ensued, many could not accept how an elite athlete (doing what must come easy) could suffer from this and quickly cast negative judgement on her motive for withdrawal. High-profile journalist Piers Morgan appeared to lead the charge on Twitter, ruthlessly accusing Biles of being a poor role model. He even published an article in the *Daily Mail* in which he said: 'Sorry, Simone Biles, but there's nothing heroic or brave about quitting because you're not having "fun" – you let down your teammates, your fans and your country.'[1]

Although shockingly inaccurate and grossly naive from a psychological perspective, Morgan's standpoint, and that of others who commented in support, was seemingly fuelled by a presumption of Simone's mindset being stable and robust. In a sense, they believed it to be immovable from delivering results, but more so impregnable to emotion, external pulls and adversity. Thus, Morgan's judgement was flawed by an assessment of how he thought someone *should* feel or act based on their occupation or level of success.

We are all guilty to varying degrees of hatching such delusions when attempting to evaluate the lives of others. It is a generalised bias we fall victim to when attempting to assess our own standing within society or a social peer group, by comparing ourselves to others as a measure to quantify our own self-worth.[2] The problem is that this discounts individual variation and uniqueness and thus underplays their/our personally held flaws, which often lie hidden under the summit of success.

The distortion of success

What is fascinating about observing elite world-class athletes at work is that we almost always fail to acknowledge that they must also have to manage their personal lives and issues. It is an often delicate balance that requires an element of emotional control and self-regulation in order to orchestrate brilliance on the biggest stages.

Arguably, as we witness such amazing feats of human ability, we appear to find it incomprehensible that successful people can also be experiencing 'everyday' personal distractions or performance inhibitors. These could be relationship problems, family concerns, or personal issues such as a temporary mental health crisis or the self-harm that often follows, like addiction.

We fall victim to two inextricable false beliefs. We equate success with happiness and naturally assume that people who have achieved a degree of success – often above ours – must have their life in order: a life of harmony, void of distraction and drama. After all, they appear to excel so effortlessly in their given field, it goes without saying that they must excel in all other aspects of their life. Right?

At the same time, if we dare to acknowledge the potential impact of external stress factors on performance, then we presume elite mindsets are in some way resilient and therefore transport such individuals through life unimpeded by external pulls. Almost as if they are so focused and mentally tough, the mundane does not matter or affect them. After all, they are hugely successful, often well known and undoubtably wealthy by default, so what is there to be stressed or depressed about?

The shock comes when someone highly successful in the public eye speaks out or gets exposed. In these moments, we are treated to a unique look into their personal lives through the unrelenting lens of media coverage. It is only then that we become aware of the fragility of their success and as a result we can relate in some way as their cloak of invincibility falls. These exceptional individuals, who are experiencing episodes of mental instability, or may have engaged in misconduct, appear to undergo a process of humanisation as their pedestal cracks.

In January 2022, the former UFC middleweight champion Robert Whittaker fought reigning UFC world champion Israel Adesanya for the second time. Although Whittaker also lost for the second time, during the post-fight press conference, UFC president Dana White commented on Whittaker's mindset during their first fight. He said, 'It was clear in their first fight that he had things going on at home, he had a poor camp and wasn't fully prepared.'

Not only did I find this admission fascinating due to the magnitude of their first fight and the stakes at play, but it highlighted that no matter who you are, or how big the occasion, negative distractions and uncontrollable external events do not discriminate. They can come at the most inappropriate times and infiltrate even the strongest minds, derailing focus and leading to poor preparation and undesired outcomes, regardless of one's status or occupation.

Yet whether we choose to admit it or not, the demise of those in such positions of privilege can afford a glimmer of hope, in some morally wrongful but comforting way – a momentary invitation for us to fantasise about the potential of our own capabilities.

I find this particularly tragic, not because we appear to revel in the downfall of others achieving more than us, but because we do not believe we are capable of such greatness until we observe the fragility in others. We believe that innate talent and good fortune belong to the 'rest' and as a consequence we never fully explore what lies dormant within ourselves.

Take my mother, for example. On the day of my first book's publication and throughout the brief media interest that ensued, she often said, 'These things don't happen to people like us.'

People like us? Why, are we not worthy?

Although repackaged, the above comment also shares this yielding assumption: 'The only way I'll be a millionaire is if I win the lottery.'

With respect, I find such statements to be a cop-out. They allude to a complete and utter lack of self-confidence and personal value, a remarkable void of self-understanding and perceived capability. They confirm a reluctance to take risks and meet adversity head on, to realise fully what these people are capable of achieving. They are afraid of failing and as a result they remain at baseline, assuring ultimate emotional comfort, where cognitive resources and behavioural output remain in first gear.

The tragedy is in failing to acknowledge the inextricable relationship between success and failure; that one cannot exist without the other. Remarkably, the box containing a world of self-discovery and possible opportunity is kept closed by our very own hands. We lock ourselves in through a lack of self-confidence and without the courage to dream big. Over time, we lose the child within us – a belief in magic and an appetite to fly – and as a result, we never believe we are ready until it is too late.

In summary

So why did I open with this chapter? For two crucial reasons that aim to tee up the main concept of this book.

First, we tend to believe that once a certain mindset has been built and calibrated to achieve success, it remains fixed, like a blueprint that has been printed in permanent marker. In reality, mindset is constantly in transit and requires discipline, sacrifice and flexibility in order to remain on point and to adapt to the ever-changing circumstances and demands of our environment.

Second, I hope to demonstrate that through hard work, commitment and 'healthy' consistency, mindset can be positively manipulated, refocused and conditioned to facilitate success.

KEY POINTS

- Challenge your beliefs. Take measured steps or plan an approach towards something that will challenge your resolve. For example, undertake the initial stages of applying for a new course, or start prepping to attend the gym, or aligning diet with training goals or lifestyle aspirations.

- If there is something you know you want to achieve, an itch that needs scratching, write it down and deconstruct it. For example, work backwards through a process of 'inverted thinking' from a visualisation of 'arriving' at the end goal and develop a strategic path back towards where you are now. Then, very slowly, start to align your behaviour and formulate the establishment of solid, consistent routines.

- Once you make a commitment, you must also make a personal pact with yourself to see it though regardless of anything. In 2016, mine was to write and publish *Becoming the 0.1%*.

- Finally, even at baseline, you are strong enough to harness the resolve to overcome hard things, develop self-confidence through tailored goal-aligned exposure, build resilience (*cognitive endurance*) and form new behavioural habits in direct alignment with your aspirations for success.

CHAPTER TWO

Mindset Development and Ability

Throughout my teenage years, from striving to become a professional rugby league player to then changing course and becoming a Royal Marines Commando, I was fascinated by the specific, albeit subjective, ingredients that make some people excel and find success among a body of like-minded and competitive talent.

What propels only a select few forward to reach that elusive, collectively held goal when, arguably, most have received the same training, engaged in the correct practices, and been exposed to the right coaches, mentors and environments?

I can vividly remember being the most talented up-and-coming player at Hunslet RLFC, who are based at South Leeds Stadium, in Leeds. That statement makes me cringe slightly, but it was the reality. I was very much a big fish in a little pond. Then I went to Leeds Rhinos in the Super League, the top level of British rugby league, and was surrounded by some remarkable examples of talent.

There was a saying back then that accounted for the vast difference in game speed, player and team cohesive ability, and overall game quality in the Super League: 'First division clubs train you to play first division, whereas Super League clubs train you to play Super League.' There was no truer reality and this was absolutely evident for a player transitioning up or down and for any spectator free from bias. Exactly the same sport, but worlds apart in every facet of the game.

Funding aside, which arguably underpinned the vast difference, it came down to the facilities, the time spent training and the quality of coaching, with specific coaches for attack, defence and other key tactical positions. Yes, the elite teams within the Super League attracted and nurtured the best, but the environment and the 'badge' (club logo) made them 30 per cent better, coupled with the techniques and strategic planning that were implemented at that level. Super League was and still is full-time, whereas first division and below are part-time.

The former two-division UFC world champion Daniel Cormier often refers to this same statistic while calling championship fights in the UFC. During his post-fight analysis, he has stated that once someone becomes a UFC champion, they automatically become 30 per cent better and this further widens the gap between the elite of the elite: the champion and the number one contender.

How is that possible? Although arguably immeasurable and thus subjective, it is undoubtedly a thing. The answer is Intrinsic Self-Confidence, the ultimate self-realising and defining moment of one's own ability and possibility, coupled with peer pressure and expectation. According to Chris Oliver, a former Royal Marines mountain leader and member of the UK Special Forces (UKSF, commonly referred to as 'the service' by those within), peer pressure plays a vital role in the UKSF: 'The company you keep is so important. The peer pressure to perform in "the service" and not let your teammates down is on another level, so we naturally out-perform anyone else for longer, as long as it takes.'

Within the Super League, some players visibly excelled. In terms of seamless ability, Danny McGuire stood alone – his body positioning, agility and balance in conjunction with ball manipulation were collectively flawless in execution. When observed in all exceptional sporting stars, such behavioural manifestations appear to embody something special, regardless of one's particular appetite for a given sporting discipline.

Brilliance ignites something beautiful within us. Whether you are into rugby, football or climbing 'free solo', for example, bias becomes null and void. When the physical is pushed by the mind to the uppermost frontiers of human capability, we often pause in admiration and wish to rewind and watch the action again.

Take tennis. I am not a huge fan, but when I watched Roger Federer playing, I was captivated. For me, Federer's sheer excellence – his masterful manipulation of body and racket – made tennis look cool and completely effortless. And yet tennis is not effortless; in fact, it is extremely difficult to play at that exalted level.

The same happened again when I watched a documentary called *Free Solo*, which saw professional climber Alex Honnold scale El Capitan's 900 metre vertical rock face at Yosemite National Park. I found myself lost for words in astonishment, and yes, I watched it multiple times over. Danny McGuire played rugby league with that same poised and composed beauty, ghosting through and manipulating the defensive line with seemingly effortless endeavour.

The million-dollar question, which lies at the very heart of this chapter, is whether he and the others were born primed with such ability and thus unbelievably fortunate to collide with their chosen sport in order to excel, or whether it was their upbringing, exposure to sport and other environmental influences.

When I interviewed the former Leeds Rhinos, GB Lions and England rugby league captain Jamie Peacock, it was clear that his strength of character was already in evidence at an early age:

I've always had a strong determination to do things. When I was nine years old, I watched the famine in Ethiopia [on the TV]. During this time everyone was taking part in charity runs and I wanted to take part and do one. The song 'Everybody Wants to Run the World' by Tears for Fears was big at the time.

However, Mum wouldn't let me do it because I was only nine, so I walked around the street trying to do metre-long steps and worked out a distance of 250 metres. I told my mum this and said, 'Mum, if I walk around the street twenty times, that's 5K, so I can do my own sponsored run!'

On this basis, Mum agreed to let me do it. I got my own sponsorship form, filled it out and got people on the street plus friends and family to donate. Then I proceeded to do the run and raised £26 for charity.

For me this just demonstrated my compassion as a kid and wanting things to be fair for others. It fucks me off when I don't see others being treated fairly, you know? Also, I suppose it demonstrated my drive and determination, even at a very young age.

It is the case that neither I nor anyone in the field of psychology can say definitively where the skeleton key to success is buried. However, I have studied what is currently known and share here my academic interpretation alongside my personal experiences and my observations from witnessing the production of successful outcomes in others.

Commando Training

After eighteen months to two years of mental, physical and psychometric testing – all under the mystical and intimidating cloak of the Royal Marines selection process – I arrived at the start of Commando Training in May 2005, ready to confront a Goliath of adversity and hardship. I began the thirty-two-week course with another fifty-eight filtered and primed recruits, all of whom had met the stringent selective guidelines. However, while some, including myself, found the resolve to venture on through the weeks, others fell away and went home (see Figure 2.1).

It is only now, through reflection and analysis, that I am able to express my opinion on the 'why and how' of what was truly a life-changing experience for all involved.

Throughout training and during the years that followed my short career in the Royal Marines, I have been fascinated with the key and subtle ingredients that facilitate cognitive performance and produce success, especially in formidable endeavours such

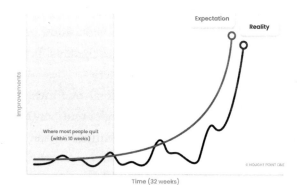

Figure 2.1 The 'expected' journey towards success vs the reality – and where the majority quit

as elite military training regimes. These elite courses embody all of life's struggles condensed and elicit the full complement of our emotional range, requiring us very quickly to learn how to self-regulate during adversity if we want to find success. Therefore, there is much to learn from elite military training regimes and their ability to transform someone's perception of their capability, and thus their ability.

Focusing on Commando Training, the first fifteen weeks resembled nothing like a young hopeful's expectation of becoming a Royal Marines Commando. The initial first phase of training (weeks one to ten) was all about pressure induced by time. Much to everyone's dismay, we were not fast-roping out of helicopters or entering buildings wearing night-vision goggles – all the 'Gucci' stuff, we call it, which attracts all those recruits with the thirst for undiluted adventure and extreme adrenaline. No, during the first ten weeks we were herded like cattle, dazed and startled, as the Training Team induced optimal panic through the application of time pressure and fear of reprisal.

The programming was so intense that recruits often had only 15–30 seconds to enter the block, change into a different set of clothing or uniform, and collectively get back outside in three ranks ready to go again. Such time frames are unattainable, of course, which invites the physical repercussions, escalating and maintaining the anxiety that feeds the gradual build-up of mental and physical fatigue.

This period is, quite frankly, horrific as one must learn to master and embed 'effective' and 'strategic' routines (*that facilitate successful outcomes*), keep such routines robust through the consistent application of self-discipline, and remain steadfast under pressure. This is all while suffering the horrific and often debilitating side effects of sleep deprivation. For example, during the first ten weeks, a recruit was lucky to get 3–4 hours' sleep a night. Some weeks, you were kept up for days on end.

To envision this reality, at the start of training, recruits must hand wash their clothes in a woefully disproportionate number of sinks per recruit: three maximum, if I remember correctly. Then dry them off in a drying room. Again, there is not enough space for everyone and if you are lucky, come the early hours, you need to start ironing ready for an early-morning inspection at 07:00 hours. This process kept the disciplined recruits up all night; the undisciplined went to bed.

And this, ladies and gentlemen, marks a subtle yet self-sabotaging moment in the distinction between one's ability to sustain performance and find success and categorical failure of the course and a ticket home. Indeed, evidence has shown that 'when presented with a choice, individuals typically pick the option that is the easiest, quickest, and most enjoyable', but when it comes to success, this 'hardwired default' is detrimental and must be overcome.[1]

This moment is the true test. A recruit has very little time to make an important and potentially life-changing decision. Do you take a huge gamble and stay, hope it gets more exciting and endure the pain, or succumb to your initial, shocking reaction and go home, with potentially severe damage to your self-esteem forever. It is a zero-sum game. Whatever you decide comes with massive implications and consequences.

Staying on the course means endless discomfort, prolonged uncertainty, heartache and panic – all the negative emotions we naturally try to avoid. Or you can leave and get immediate emotional relief, *but* you have categorically failed. For me, there was only one way forward: to remain on task, put up with it all and finish the job. As my dad always said: 'Finish what you start.'

There is no innate talent or ability required that will predict success on the Royal Marines Commando course, only a series of simple choices that carry huge consequences. Quite frankly, those that do not apply self-discipline at the very start miss the window of opportunity to embed the behavioural routines necessary to assure intensive skills absorption. Failure to do so makes them fall behind and eventually exit the course. Remarkably, though, you cannot see this at the time.

There is such an internal conflict at play here. Logic informs any recruit that the right thing to do is to complete all your personal admin – washing, drying, ironing, cleaning and polishing – at the end of a very intense working day, in order to ensure you pass inspection the next morning. The kicker is that you may have had only 2–4 hours' sleep the previous night and the temptation to lie down on your bed and go to sleep is massive – rather like a fly being enticed to its death by a fluorescent lamp. Finding the resolve in this moment and keeping it consistent throughout the first ten weeks requires massive mental toughness, which can be conditioned only by going through this process and learning to trust it.

Alternatively, once the day is finished and the Training Team have gone home, you could choose to relax, spend hours on the phone to your family or watch a movie and go to bed at about 19:00 hours, aiming to sleep until the early hours and then get up prior to troop reveille at 05:00 hours to do your admin then.

This sounds wise, but it is the soft option and very quickly becomes unsustainable, in fact catastrophic when looking back through reflection and analysis. For example, getting up before 05:00 hours to do your washing, drying and ironing will wake up some, if not all, of the block and one thing you cannot do is sabotage anyone's sleep during training.

So what happens if you don't subscribe to the new cultural norms and expectations but instead decide not to accept short-term discomfort by going to bed thinking your admin can be done later? First, you quickly fall out of favour with your fellow recruits and become isolated. And second, you consistently fail inspections and the repercussions add even more fatigue and pressure. Over a period of time this leaves you constantly on the back foot as you fall further and further behind the pack.

I have often wondered how it was that eleven of the original recruits and I were able to reach the end of Commando Training – earning the coveted Green Beret – when the other forty-eight recruits did not make it. Yes, injury played a cruel part for some, but it was not that great a saboteur. I don't know the statistics, but for the majority, their progress was often cut short by their own hands. What I can attest to is that those of us who were remaining at the end appeared to have a greater fear of abject failure.

The notion of quitting filled me with feelings of incompetence and of not being good enough, coupled with the external perception of what others would think about me, especially those at home who had doubted me from the start. Everything about quitting was negative and for that reason I simply could not accept it or entertain it. The only comfort I had to control the uncontrollable was that I knew I wouldn't quit. Therefore, by not entertaining such a notion, I eventually gained an emerging and self-assured grasp of my own capability – a rare understanding that enabled me to trust myself explicitly during arduous and odds-stacked challenges. This was the secret weapon to achieving success for both myself and the remaining recruits.

We all had something to prove, not only to others but to ourselves. We had to slay the inner demon that wielded the mental weapon of unworthiness and the self-projected notion of inability. The main driver was the anticipated perception of abject failure cast on us by others, but there was something more significant in our desire to succeed: the internal representation of failure of the self – in other words, our self-concept.

The big question is, what is happening in that deeper place within our psychology that makes us place greater value on our perception of ourselves? Is this there at birth or does it turn from a flicker to a flame as we grow up?

Revelations from 'separated' twin studies

One subject that continues to spark interest in the world of psychology is the origin and make-up of development and success. At the core of the discussion is the nature vs nurture debate. Are we born with certain genetic traits that inform the construct of our intelligence, mindset and outlook, or are we shaped through our culture, experiences and exposure to specific environments, such as the quality of staff interactions and facilities?

The short answer is that everything is so intertwined, it is impossible to disentangle.[2] However, historical research studies looking at identical twins separated at birth (adopted through welfare organisations) have revealed some interesting findings in relation to the genetic predisposition vs the environmental factors argument and the emergence of intelligence.[3]

By studying adopted twins who shared 100 per cent of their genes but did not share the same environment, psychologists have been able to determine that genes account for 80 per cent of variability in intellectual ability and around 20 per cent is due to the environment.[4] However, there are two key problems with this assumption, which are very important to acknowledge.

First, twins are rarely separated at birth and usually spend the majority of their developmental stages together, whether with family members or foster carers.[5] What is more, identical twins often get mistaken for one another; they are frequently dressed the same, sleep in the same bedroom for longer and are treated similarly by others.[6] In other words, identical twins share much the same environment, as they are seen by others to be indistinguishable and thus require matching needs and preferences. So, the distribution of percentages stated above might be closer to equal than we think.

Second, and this is central to my argument, one's degree of intelligence does not always translate to drive, aspiration and success. What is intelligence anyway? Are IQ tests really the truest assessment of one's cognitive capability and the determining predictor in one's chances of being successful in life? After all, IQ tests can be practised and with practice one can achieve a better score. Surely that is not measuring baseline intellect, only knowledge at any given time.

In recent years, some psychologists have argued that intelligence, or a person's effectiveness within the social world, should be gauged on their ability to adapt quickly to change when exposed to new people or cultures and, importantly, their ability to learn how to thrive in these new and contrasting environments. So, is the answer to greater capability one's propensity to seek exposure in order to excel? With this in mind, let's take a deeper look at the effect of dedicated exposure and deliberate practice – a fundamental influence that I believe is vital to any potential genetic advancement and shaping of mindset.

For decades, scientists have studied the potential origin of success through the lens of innate predisposition, the influence of environment and the impact on performance to produce successful outcomes. Despite exhausting what is available to measure in terms of psychological research, it would appear that preparation and exposure, or deliberate practice, trump innate talent.

I wrote about the 10,000-hour rule in *Becoming the 0.1%* (Chapter 10: Achieving Mastery). According to Malcolm Gladwell in his bestselling book *Outliers*,[7] 'The closer psychologists look at the careers of the gifted, the smaller the role innate talent seems to play, and the bigger the role preparation seems to play.' He asserted that through deliberate practice or prolonged exposure to any sporting or profession-related discipline, a person would reach the ever-elusive level of mastery in their chosen craft upon achieving 10,000 hours of practice.

During the early 1990s, psychologist K. Anders Ericsson[8] studied the violinists at Berlin's Elite Academy of Music. He and his fellow researchers divided an elite pool of the world's best violinists into three groups. Group One were deemed excellent, tipped to become world-class violinists. Group Two were regarded as extremely competent but not exceptional. Group Three was made up of those considered to be good but who would never play professionally and instead would likely make excellent music teachers.[9]

Once divided, all individuals across the three groups were asked the same question: 'Over the course of your entire career, ever since you first picked up the violin, how many hours have you practised?'

Remarkably, all the violinists started playing the instrument around the age of five years. During those tender years, everyone practised roughly the same amount of time, about 2–3 hours per week. However, at around eight years old, some started to excel. Those that would eventually end up in Group One practised more: 'six hours a week by age nine, eight hours a week by age twelve, sixteen hours a week by age fourteen, and up and up.'[10]

By the age of twenty, the elite among the elite had amassed the 10,000 hours benchmark required to become exceptional, via the application of purposeful and single-minded behavioural output for over thirty hours a week, with the sole intention of getting better. This included playing the violin, reading music, visualisation, strength training in the fingers and upper limb regions, and so on. By contrast, those in Group Two had totalled 8,000 hours by twenty years old and Group Three slightly north of 4,000 hours.[11]

In summary

Now, I am not trying to say that innate talent in any manifestation is not important, of course it is, but nothing can compete with relentless drive and determination, with hard work being the long and often painstaking road, not the shortcut. Hopefully, as the above example illustrates beautifully, it is about the application of self-discipline to uphold the consistency to safeguard strategic routines and habits. It is about being relentless in your pursuit of success and in doing so learning to trust the mundane process only afforded through the benefit of experience, which will inevitably lead to the end goal.

Above all, it is about doing what others will not do – what they can't be bothered to do – that eventually enables you to do what they can no longer dream about because the gap has grown too much, albeit in the most subtle of ways.

KEY POINTS

- The barrier to establishing intrinsic self-belief and confidence and thus realising your true capability and potential is your reluctance to step outside of your comfort zone and seek the right exposures.

- It is vital to seek exposure to the right aspirational vehicles – environments, people and experiences – the specific and unique demands or situations that create behavioural adaptation and facilitate personal change, aligning and paving the way to your desired destination.

- When presented with choices, we are hardwired to select the quickest, easiest and most enjoyable option. Such biased choice selection is often in dire conflict with the hardship we must endure to realise success. Choose wisely.

- Deliberate practice and preparation trump innate talent.

- You are the barrier to greatness. Nothing else.

CHAPTER THREE

The Reality of Mindset

My interpretation of the construct and fragility of what we define as elite mindsets is only possible by reflecting upon my own experience while undertaking Royal Marines Commando Training. What I can say is that my mental resilience became more robust as the requirements of training became ever more demanding. In this sense, as the intensity increased, I was forced to adapt my mindset, making me mentally tougher and more confident that I could come through the hard times. In short, through personal desire, I adapted to withstand environmental requirements.

As a result of prolonged exposure to incredibly gruelling physical training, I reached an unimaginable state of mental capability. The culmination of this was tested to its utmost while I was completing the Commando Tests, and even more so in finding the resolve to get through the final test, the infamous 30-miler.[1]

The Royal Marines Commando Tests mark the beginning of the end of training, a truly horrific period for any recruit. The Tests comprise four of the hardest physical and mentally challenging tasks in the world and must be completed within five days. They are as follows:

- **The Endurance Course**: This six-mile course begins with a two-mile run across Woodbury Common, Devon, while navigating various obstacles, including tight tunnels, pipes, wading pools and the infamous 'sheep dip', all while carrying 21lbs of full fighting order (*webbing*) plus weapon: the SA80. After the two-mile first section, it is a four-mile run back to camp, where a recruit must get six out of ten shots on target to pass the course successfully in under seventy-two minutes.
- **The 9-mile Speed March**: Again carrying full fighting order plus weapon, recruits run/walk as a troop at a pace of ten minutes per mile in order to complete the test in under ninety minutes.
- **The Tarzan Assault Course**: On this high aerial 1.5 kilometre assault course, a recruit must navigate through and negotiate technical obstacles and transitions under immense fatigue while carrying full fighting order and personal weapon system in under thirteen minutes.
- **The 30-miler:** This is the final test that stands between a recruit and the Green Beret. It is a thirty-mile hike, run across wild, uneven and open moorland on Dartmoor. Recruits carry up to 50lbs of fighting order and safety equipment plus weapon, and the test must be completed in eight hours.

Training to undertake these tasks in isolation is one thing, but a recruit arrives at the Tests completely exhausted, with eight months and the previous years in preparation all taking their toll on the body. Many start the Tests with significant injuries, such

as stress fractures in the lower limbs, ankle injuries
and pelvic issues from training constantly with and
carrying weight. Not to mention horrific blisters, the
loss of toenails and ligament damage. It is a true and
raw test of personal resolve and a vibrant desire to
succeed.

By this stage of training, I was exhausted mentally and physically and was carrying an ACL rupture in my left knee and
a slight tear in my right Achilles tendon. Yet I had reached a
level of mental capacity that propelled me forward despite my
debilitating physical injuries.

My mindset, come the end of training, was due to an environmental adaptation to exposure (*Royal Marines training*) and
I can say with a degree of confidence that it was not due solely
to innate predisposition, if at all. But here is the major revelation: once I finished training and the demand stimulus ceased,
so too did the optimal capability of my mindset. That finely
tuned weapon soon lost its edge. As a result, I no longer had the
ability nor the appetite to push myself continually through the
pain barrier and withstand the level of suffering, at least to that
extent, that I had been forced to endure in order to complete
Commando Training.

Looking back now at this raw and intensive period of my
life, I have been able to arrive at the following personal conclu-
sions about mindset.

First, upholding the finely tuned element of mindset requires
an extremely strong and personal stimulus. A goal or ambition
that is made non-negotiable in order to maintain focus and to
apply the self-discipline required to uphold consistency, without fail, even when motivation strays. Second, once acquired

and aligned for specific success or goal acquisition, the mindset capability is not eternally rigid once you reach a certain level of proficiency.

Just like physical fitness and conditioning, the mind requires constant maintenance and alignment via the application and exposure to hardship conditioning. Midway through training, I remember thinking that by the end and on reaching the Commando Tests, I would surely have no doubts about my ability or feel nervous before the start of each Test. Therefore, I didn't really worry about them, as I thought I would be so mentally hardened by that point that I would not be fazed.

In reality, prior to each Test, I was desperately trying to keep a lid on my emotional alarm bells. On the surface I probably looked composed, but anyone observing me closely while I tried to eat breakfast the morning of each Test would have said otherwise. I was so nervous that I had to force the food down, one mouthful of cooked breakfast followed by one large gulp of water to wash it all down.

When you think about it for a second, why had this emotional response not been eliminated by now – through conditioning – given I had arrived at the end of training? After all, within a matter of days I would almost certainly become one of the world's elite and most highly regarded and feared soldiers. How could I possibly be so anxious about these physical tests when I had been primed during the previous eight months for the raw reality of combat operations?

The truth is, at the start of the Endurance Course – the first Commando Test – I was so nervous that my legs were trembling and felt hollow. Other lads were being sick. I was carrying so much self-doubt. On the one hand, I believed I could do it – I had learned that no matter how hard it got, I would never quit, so that gave me an element of comfort. On the other hand, I was talking myself out of it. What if I am physically fatigued and once under way I just can't get going? What if I have eaten too much or too little this morning? What if I haven't eaten enough in the previous days and I become exhausted?

All this was flooding my mind on the biggest stage, where onlookers would naturally presume I was completely in control, mentally solid and, to a large degree, mentally conditioned to the environment and demand (war and conflict). As such, I assumed that exposure and experience would in some way make me unemotional to adversity and fear. The reality could not have been further from the truth. I just learned to handle my emotions better via an emotional skills foundation or understanding. The outcome of hardship exposure. (More on this in Chapter 9.)

The pressure to pass the test alone was enough to give you a terrible night's sleep, if you managed to get a second at all. Then on the morning itself, it was like waking up in hell. As soon as my eyes opened, I was hit instantly with, 'Oh, my god!' Despite this, I had to get up, prep, weigh my kit and make the four-mile speed march up to the notorious Woodbury Common to start the damn thing at 07:30 hours.

As the first three recruits set off, I felt sick to my stomach. Once they had departed, the stack moved forward in sections of three or four, nearer to the start line. As my component moved closer, I felt horrendous. Once we set off, I can remember running like I was in slow motion, in a sense of complete disbelief at what was happening. You could say it was a form of shock. I ran frantically as I negotiated the two-mile gruelling obstacle course across the common against the clock. Thankfully, I felt okay from a cardiovascular perspective, strong in the legs and very good mentally as a result. In fact, my physical response to the course as I progressed through it gave me the mental confidence and this grew and grew.

Once I had completed the two-mile cross-country section, it was a four-mile best effort (*all out*) run back to camp. This was also frantic as I ran wet-through, my boots squelching to the brim with water and covered in muck and stinking sludge, trying desperately to arrive at Commando Training Centre under the allotted time: seventy-two minutes.

Upon finishing the 30-miler, the final Commando Test, I had completed training successfully and earned my coveted Green Beret. I felt such a huge sense of accomplishment, coupled with the mixed emotions of putting to bed what had felt like a lifetime's nightmare.

Although the initial few weeks were probably the most satisfying and fulfilled I have ever experienced from a professional and goal-acquisition perspective, it did not feel like I thought it would to become a Royal Marines Commando. Sadly, the euphoria of the achievement soon became a distant memory and it was not long before I began the process of soul-searching yet again.

Being in a position of privilege sparked a very strange conflict within me. Among the Marines I never felt special and, if I am perfectly honest, I was quite underwhelmed by the whole experience post-training. However, once I re-entered 'civvy street' during leave periods, I thrived on the attention. I fully lived up to the role and the expectation that my friends, family and others had as to how a Royal Marine would act. But that is exactly what it was … an act.

I used the title as a protective and somewhat intimidating shield, not to be threatening as such but to uphold my reputation, massage the expectations of others and endorse the embodiment of the Royal Marines. Inside, I was the same old Gareth, the accomplishment of training fast becoming a distant memory and the mindset no longer that finely tuned.

This is such an important consideration when we look at the mindset of others whom we wish to emulate. Yes, such people will have been through unbelievable training and conditioning and have undertaken thousands of hours of deliberate practice to excel in their chosen field. However, no matter who we are, we all have our off days. We must negotiate external issues sensitively in order to maintain consistency and performance.

But more so, we become accustomed to our surroundings and they become the norm. It does not take long to take such acquired privilege for granted, which in turn opens the door to complacency. Crucially, this often requires someone to act the part in order to uphold the external facade, masking their internal thoughts and feelings to appease the expectations of others.

According to psychologists, we are all actors and perform in ways that are expected of us in different social situations.[2] This need for us to act in certain ways is driven by the societal background in which we have been raised. For example, how we engage with a shop assistant is different from how we might behave when seeing a doctor, or how we conduct ourselves in church. Such examples require us to 'act out' a certain script, known as a 'social schema', in which we apply self-regulation to align our behaviour with an expectation of emotional expression.

Take the role of coaching a team: that is an act. Being a judge: that is an act, and so on. Let's face it, how many times have you not felt right on a particular day when you have had meetings or other front-facing responsibilities and you have had to tell yourself, 'Game face on.' What is that? That's acting.

We often rely on these acting roles and crucially see them as the embodiment of the individual, but that can be damaging.

It fails to acknowledge the emotions that make us human, discounting the real person behind the mask, and thus underplays our inherent fragility while trying to conform with social expectations and responsibilities.

Therefore, when it comes to the external expectation of those with perceived elite thinking and behaviour, a problem occurs that creates a discrepancy between what is possible at any given moment. For instance, on any given day, an individual may be trying to hold it together due to a multitude of factors – life away from work, a loss of self-confidence, a lack of sleep or fatigue. Yet the observer often fails to consider these issues that can affect us all.

Somehow, because of our perception of elite mindsets and the success that they can produce, we view them as being like an iron cloak protecting high-achieving individuals from vulnerability, stress and mental illness. We believe that underneath the armour exists harmony, underpinned by health, happiness and financial security.

The reality could not be further from the truth.

This delicate internal versus external ambivalence opens the door to cognitive derailment, a conflict we try desperately to appease at both ends. Ultimately, this leads to exhaustion and disillusionment, igniting the touch paper that can lead to debilitating mental issues, which hamper if not halt consistent performance outcomes.

Therefore, while anyone can take steps to manipulate and align mindset to produce successful outcomes, conversely, without adequate care and a holistic approach to emotional care and attentional restoration, our wellbeing can become negatively affected.

KEY POINTS

- Mindset is fluid, conditioned and maintained through environmental demands. Once the demand stimulus has ended, so too does the optimisation of its capability.

- Regardless of who we are or what job we undertake, our emotions are hardwired and thus require constant regulation and self-control. Exposure and conditioning cannot override this hardwiring; we just become better at managing our emotions with experience. Anxiety, self-doubt and fear are always there, chipping away at us and waiting to sabotage our success by inhibiting our ability to realise our full potential.

- No matter what level of success we acquire in life, we become accustomed to it. The magic dust soon wears off and we are left with familiarity and the mundane, which opens the door to complacency.

- We are all social actors. We act the moment we leave the safety of our homes. When the acting begins to create internal conflict due to an inability to uphold external expectation, it can become detrimental to cognitive functioning and lead to mental health issues.

- Behind the sum of identity lies a human being striving to hold it together to perform, fuelled by the nature of their social role and the expectations of others.

The Seven Phases of Mindset

So, how can we perform better for longer while upholding our mental wellbeing?

The following seven chapters aim to highlight the fluidity of the elite mindset via seven phases. By no means do these account for the complexity of thought, feeling or emotional response at any given time, but they demonstrate that motivation is not always present and mental resilience is susceptible to penetration if abused.

The path towards continued success is neither guaranteed nor fixed once a specific prescription of thinking and behavioural alignment has been achieved. In order to maximise performance and safeguard our mental health, there is work to be done to sustain the delicate connection between elite thinking and the desired behavioural application while trying to mitigate a fall into burnout. Without due care and attention, the journey can take its toll on mental wellbeing. But by understanding that a success mindset is adaptable, fluid and susceptible and requires constant self-care and attention, it can be conditioned to deliver the results you desire.

CHAPTER FOUR

Phase One: Cultivating Mental Toughness

Before we proceed, you will never operate at your full potential without first defining and then pursuing your 'intrinsic purpose', while also knowing your true value. From a personal perspective, cultivating and fortifying mental toughness while extending the baseline of mental resilience requires three key ingredients:

- exposure to environments

- the benefit of time and familiarity

- the power of experience.

Exposure to environments

There was nothing I hated more in training and as a fully trained Royal Marines Commando than going in the field, away from base, on exercises on Woodbury Common, Salisbury Plain, Dartmoor and remote parts of Scotland. It was as raw and deprived as it gets in terms of living conditions, especially in training; even more so during the harsh winter months, when we were completely exposed to the elements, living on military rations and having to operate day and night on limited to no sleep.

These exercises were a persistent attack on your motivation and resolve. The field made you question everything, especially during the first fifteen weeks of training, when they were carefully orchestrated to weed out those recruits with vulnerable mental strength and determination.

Life in the field rarely lasted longer than a week, but at times it was a minute-by-minute struggle to stay positive. The environmental manipulation imposed by the Training Team made you doubt your life choices at every turn as they extracted all the convenience, comfort and joy out of your existence. I dreaded leaving camp, as did many others, and as the days drew closer to our departure, I would start to retreat within myself. I was filled with trepidation, while desperately trying to find positives in the impending reality that I had to face in order to achieve my end goal.

Training epitomised the embodiment of delayed gratification, with success determined by doing what you did not want to do (day in, day out) – something that went against every fibre of your being – but it was a necessity that the few successful acknowledged was worth the suffering and sacrifice to reap the rewards come the end of that endeavour.

During my time in Royal Marines training, the exposure to the extreme demands posed by the CTCRM (Commando Training Centre Royal Marines), and the strict disciplinary requirements needed to transform a civilian into an elite soldier, helped to condition my body. More importantly, they helped to construct my mindset, an internal cognitive adjustment to environmental exposure that made me more mentally robust. It enabled me to adapt with limited anguish and to push further through the changing seasons, from the heat of summer into the cold winter months.

Much research has been done on what is called the 'mere exposure effect' and how the more time one spends in a particular environmental setting (such as Royal Marines Training or any other high-intensity, performance-driven environment) elicits biological adaptations. For example, look at Kenyan runners, who make up only 0.06 per cent of the world's population but produce so many record breakers, despite many of their training facilities being very poor. How do they do it? Quite simply, they train at altitude (2400m above sea level). This creates more red blood cells, the body's clever modification to counter the lack of oxygen, which in turn delivers more red blood cells faster to the muscles.[1] Therefore, when they return to sea level, they have a natural performance edge increasing aerobic capacity, lactic acid tolerance and oxygen flow to the muscles. That is why so many UFC fighters, boxers and other athletes also train at altitude.

In preparation for deployments to Afghanistan, one of the most inhospitable places in the world in which to operate, Royal Marines would first spend three months in Norway. In this Arctic environment, in direct contrast to the Afghan summer, Commandos had to fine-tune their behaviour and administration to remain combat effective in sub-zero temperatures. They did this by practising artificial light discipline during the dark, maintaining personal kit and weapons, and constantly adapting to the conditions to counter the debilitating effects of cold weather exposure and frostbite. Unbelievably, this bitterly cold environment prepared the Royal Marines for operations in Afghanistan. It hardened their resolve, but it did not end there. Afterwards, they deployed to Oman for environmental and acclimatisation training, prior to crossing over into Afghanistan.

In the examples above, the psychological advantages gained are both rich and fundamental. The mere exposure effect to such environments can elicit physiological adaptations. It improves self-discipline, develops better habits related to success and nurtures self-regulation – the ability to manage our emotions during adversity. Positive mindset adjustments facilitated via the process of exposure, while absorbing the benefits of environmental familiarity and thus safeguard the transfer of performance.[2]

At the very start of Commando Training, the mere thought of undertaking the Tests had not only overwhelmed me but filled me with anxiety – it had felt like an impossible, incomprehensible venture. Yet as I progressed through the thirty-two-week course, I and the others established new routines that were essential. We kept adapting to the cultural environment – the expectations and standards of the Royal Marines known as the Cultural DNA. This meant the quick implementation and continual tweaking of behavioural alignment to facilitate success.

Cultural DNA

It could be argued that elite working environments have strong 'cultural DNA': a collection of social and cultural instructions that individuals, teams or troops live by, which inform growth, development, collective functioning and efficiency.

The Cultural Architects

These are the trusted members of the group. They help build and maintain the ethos by constantly evaluating the current state of the culture at any given time. The positive: an environment that encourages people to go the extra mile, to give support without the assurance of it being returned. The negative: there could be certain people who are negative influences or do not conform.

For example, at Leeds Rhinos, no one was allowed to celebrate a PB (personal best) in the gym. Why? Because it was deemed one's responsibility to perform and strive for excellence and not bask in self-adulation. That is an example of how effective Cultural Architects can be in eliciting 'introverted' performance outcomes.

The Cultural Assassins

These are selected to find weaknesses, to try to sabotage the culture, to rock the boat and disrupt group harmony. In Royal Marines training, the Training Team were all Cultural Assassins at various stages. For the first fifteen weeks of training, they tried to break down the troops' morale and trust, thus inviting personal disillusionment and collective paranoia. It was up to the recruits who stayed on the course to find resolve, adapt and continually re-establish harmony by upholding the cultural architecture and in doing so invite the onset of resilience and collective trust.

Cultural Assassins are sometimes naturally occurring. How often have you heard the phrase

'People always slip through the net'? These people are toxic and must be rooted out immediately to restore harmony. For example, midway through Royal Marines training, one of the section leaders was asked about a particular recruit. He replied, 'He's not one of us, he must go – naturally talented, yes, but personal attitude and application, no.' Within a week, the recruit was weeded out.

The benefit of time and familiarity

The fortification of mindset can become established only via a further key component: the benefit of time. For the few recruits that succeeded at CTCRM, we gave ourselves the benefit of time to reap the subtle and emotionally calming effects of environmental and cultural familiarity. What had initially felt like an overwhelmingly raw and harrowing environment became a place of familiarity; towards the end of training it even felt like home in some way, as if we had been there a lifetime.

Resisting the knee-jerk reaction to pack and head home delivered an element of perverse comfort and, in the most subtle of ways, started to reinforce our self-confidence. With each day engaged in the process, we grew stronger and the oppressive, intimidating effects of CTCRM began to become more hospitable as we adapted to the cultural expectations.

As a result, and over time, what had once seemed like an impossible undertaking began to appear doable, at the very least. Sadly, those that left the course suddenly did not allow themselves enough time to adjust emotionally and gain the comfort of familiarity.

The power of experience

Withstanding the initial emotional onslaught elicited by the CTCRM, we began a process of alignment with our environment, which unknowingly was facilitating the best chances of success. Time and understanding slowly relieved the unnerving effects of the new environment and thus elevated self-confidence in the process, allowing the privilege of experience to grow – appeasing the effects of anxiety – which was vital.

Why? Well, over a period of going through the hard times of physical training and sleep deprivation, we learned that these tough challenges did not last and we could come through them. For example, I discovered that I could still perform while enduring the effects of severe sleep deprivation and that I could find the resolve to continue going forward during horrendous load carries across rugged terrain. If I felt like I wanted to go home and my motivation had waned, I knew that it was only a temporary mental state. With a semi-decent sleep, I would be back on point, focused and raring to go again.

Therefore, gaining this wealth of experience in adverse situations allowed me to make more rational and informed decisions when times got tough. Basically, it established composure through self-understanding. This privilege allowed a window into the deepest, often unexplored avenues of my mind and allowed me to get to know myself fully – what I liked and disliked at either end of the comfort vs discomfort spectrum.

Why was this so vital? Well, it not only allowed me to prepare for the worst possible outcomes mentally, affording me a better chance of success in truly gruelling situations, but I had been there before. I had confronted the negative self-talk and crucially had come through it with practice, which was invaluable. Therefore, with time and experience in the thick of adversity, my nervous energy began to settle. I was becoming mentally conditioned and learning how to self-regulate, which mitigated any panic I might have felt through an emerging sense of anxiety about the unknown.

The Irish mixed martial artist Conor McGregor once said the following about entering the boxing gym as a child and the mental conditioning he underwent in order to massage his nerves:

When I was a kid, I realised I was getting these nerves, I would sit back and analyse these weird emotions. Ultimately, that is what drove me towards combat sports, in order to be able to manage those emotions ... So every time I would go to a boxing gym, I would feel those butterflies that I felt that time and I'd be thinking, yes, now I'm getting more comfortable, now I'm feeling these feelings more. So the more I feel them, the more I'm going to be comfortable in them. So I always searched for that feeling ... and now I'm fighting in the MGM Grand [Garden Arena, Las Vegas]![3]

That is the epitome of mindset alignment and reinforcement through environmental conditioning. It is a mental approach by which time and experience allow one to learn that consistent exposure and application eventually deliver rewards and in doing so, teach you how to manage your emotions during change and adversity.

By virtue of acknowledging the ups and downs – the uncertain and adverse process of goal or career acquisition – and by buying into it, you uncover your secret weapon, not available to those who reside in their comfort zone. It is 'intrinsic self-confidence': the rare type of confidence that requires no external praise or validation when evaluating risk and embarking on challenges.

As Commando recruits in training, we reached a point where we knew, absolutely without question, that we could come through the hard times. No matter what additional obstacles were thrown at us, we could find the inner strength and resolve to overcome them without the help of others. Basically, we developed 'self-agency', a sense of utmost emotional control, a capacity to influence our thoughts and behaviour and have faith in our ability to back ourselves in any situation.

We were psychologically stable yet flexible in the face of adversity, and by trusting the process we knew that it would ultimately pay dividends. The adversity would end (temporarily) and small wins would become available, subtle enough to uphold our desire and motivation to continue.

Lesson 1

Leaving the comfort zone

So how does one acquire the Commando mindset without undertaking the extremes of Commando Training?

Building and reinforcing mindset is in part due to redefining someone's perceived understanding of their own capability. In a nutshell, it is that simple. However, this is only possible by leaving your comfort zone. So, what is a comfort zone?

For me, the term refers to a mental living space that affords emotional safety and familiarity. It is an imaginary safe house that acts to protect us against any form of emotional risk and the adverse effects of challenge and external opinion, for example when encountering the perceived negative connotations of failure. However, although it may protect our self-confidence by providing a comfort blanket, it comes with hidden shackles, restricting personal development, self-discovery and growth. Therefore, it inhibits people from realising their full and true potential.

Learning to think and alter your behaviour to produce different results and sustained outcomes is a complex undertaking. It requires a synchronised interplay between the mind and the transfer of thought into physical action, known as 'behavioural enactment'. This is achieved through exposure to the specific environments that produce experience for long enough to form new habits and thus facilitate the desired success.

Therefore, laying the foundations to ensure aspirational alignment requires an individual to step outside their realm of emotional safety, often referred to as the comfort zone. Taking the bold leap to leave it often invites a degree of adversity as our emotions are challenged, sparking the instinctive reaction to consider stepping back inside it. Much of this cognitive default is due to what is called 'loss aversion bias', a psychological phenomenon where people perceive the risk of potential loss or energy investment to be greater than the reward and so remain shackled in the illusion of psychological comfort.[4]

This bias has evolutionary origins and once preserved energy and safeguarded survival during the hunter-gatherer period. However, that cognitive mechanism has no benefit in contemporary goal or career advancement, therefore it must be acknowledged as a fundamental risk factor and manually overridden through enactment and exposure. Do not fall victim to this bias!

By gaining composure with the benefit of time and experience to find the resolve necessary to come through adverse situations, you will plant the seeds of intrinsic self-confidence. By undergoing this process and learning to trust it, the seeds will grow strong roots, creating solid foundations that will further reinforce and assure your self-belief. This will pave a trusted path from the comfort zone onto greater levels of self-exploration, personal development and growth. Therefore, establishing a goal acquisition strategy to leave the realms of comfort is essential.

Historically, I have always deconstructed large and overwhelming complex goals in two ways. First, I ask myself what systematic preparation is required to hit the base of the journey and put the right foundations in place in order to give myself the best shot at completing the first stages of the undertaking. Focus here has been only on surviving the start of a challenge. I have blocked out the bigger picture, as at that point it is irrelevant.

In this sense, I have offset the anxiety elicited by uncertainty and the potential notion of failure by buying into the implementation of attention to detail and kept it consistent through uncompromising self-discipline. In doing so, I have controlled all the available controllables, assuring me the best chances of success.

I must stress, in all my large endeavours, I have never felt assured of being successful. I have just prepared well mentally and physically and let exposure, time and experience do the rest.

Second, I mentally projected forwards to the very end of the goal: visualising the benefits and opportunities that would be on offer. Crucially, and this is key, I have finally deconstructed the undertaking – through a process of inverted thinking – all the way to the start to prepare myself mentally to come to terms with the commitment and sacrifice required.

Acknowledging and accepting the sacrifice is truly vital to prepare the mind for the task ahead, and by adhering to this process, this approach has always delivered success. If you do not mentally accept the sacrifice, however, your endeavour will probably fail.

Consistent future performance outcomes are possible only via the investment in tailored, short-term behavioural enactment. A regimented process of daily management underpinned by sacrifice and reinforced by self-discipline that acts to extinguish old habits and formulate new ones akin to the desired aspiration of success.

This process aligns the tracks, putting an individual on a journey of personal development, which at some point starts to offer increased life chances – promotion, potentially more financial freedom and, hopefully, greater levels of personal fulfilment.

The daily resilience investment

From experience, building mental resilience and the strength to push through mental boundaries – nurturing self-confidence that reverberates into all aspects of your life – is possible only through exposure to challenging physical exercise and mentally controlled challenges. The type that make you question what you are doing in the moment and whether you can find the resolve to complete the task at hand – for instance, climbing a mountain while having to overcome severe weather conditions, or exposure to hard fitness classes in order to develop mental resilience (cognitive endurance) and learn how to overcome negative self-talk, learn how to self-relate emotions and develop self-confidence.

These hard sessions and challenges can make us all nervous despite our experience, but such exposures facilitate an opportunity to learn to self-regulate our emotions. By constantly exposing yourself to this micro-process of mental discomfort, while pushing your boundaries and learning to control negative self-talk – even for one hour per day – you start to build mental toughness. This could be engaging in high-intensity training, preparation for an event or competition, or building up to and summiting a mountain peak.

Stepping outside of your comfort zone, and nurturing emotional resolve to manage discomfort, not only conditions the mind but can make your life easier through the construct of intrinsic self-confidence. During a thirty-minute high-intensity workout, for example, the body is telling the mind it cannot sustain the output and mentally you arrive at a point where you want to stop the discomfort – but you must not surrender. Under extreme stress and discomfort, we all want to quit. Deep fatigue cracks our external façade, revealing the inner vulnerability we try desperately to hide. Take comfort in knowing that 'negative thoughts of quitting are normal. They don't mean you are weak. They represent your mind trying to protect you'.[5]

It is an illusion known as 'the 40 per cent rule', which claims that when we first feel fatigued and think we must stop, we are at only 40 per cent exertion (the first pain barrier). Therefore, it is imperative that we ignore these emotional alarm bells and push through the pain.[6] Over a period of repetition, this begins to instil confidence in the self. It develops trust and an understanding whereby you know you can back your own ability to overcome adversity via the controlled experience of living through tough times. This enables you to handle all other forms of adversity that life throws at you. It is a process of concurrent physical and mental conditioning, which enables you to handle all other forms of adversity that life throws at you.

Resilience days and the practice of delayed gratification

Resilience days (*specific training sessions or challenges*) could be planned and built into each week. Periods where the mind is pushed to the limits through challenging physical activity that requires continuous internal dialogue, and the willpower to come through hard, albeit short, times. For example, Tuesdays and Thursdays could be your resilience days, which could include exposure to high-intensity workouts. These could involve selecting the harder sessions on the daily programming, choosing heavier weights than those stipulated on the programming, working at RX or RX+ (recommended exertion in CrossFit), or doing extras once the session has finished.

Subjecting yourself to the tougher option on some days, having to come to terms with this mentally and resisting the urge to cancel or simply go through the motions, will reverberate into all aspects of your life.

To support this notion, a study conducted by researchers Hare and Camerer derived from the Stanford Marshmallow Experiment[7] subjected participants to two options that were assessed by Functional Magnetic Resonance Imaging (fMRIs). Option one was to accept a greater financial reward at a later date, post the study completion, as opposed to option two, which was accepting a smaller financial reward upon the immediate conclusion of the study.

Those who chose option one – the mentally harder option – were found to develop greater resilience, self-control and discipline. More importantly, those who 'delayed gratification' (again, choosing option one) by taking the tougher route were found to be more successful in all areas of life when re-evaluated in 2011.[8] Ultimately by resisting the urge for immediate gratification, this arguably demonstrates how the constructs of mental toughness can be cultivated via the selection of our everyday choices.

Delayed gratification is the act of resisting the impulse to take immediate reward, which goes against human nature. As a human being, we want instant results. The art of trusting the process, however, is underpinned by the notion of delayed gratification: that at some point in the future, through one's ability to self-regulate and apply self-control, greater rewards will become available.

Once you learn with time and experience to trust the process, not only will you find the blueprint to success but it will keep you on track through attentional fatigue, disillusionment and periods of uncertainty, because through experience you will learn that the investment eventually pays off.

PRACTICAL APPLICATIONS

- Take small steps to build mental strength. Doing too much too soon without a period of mental and physical conditioning can be detrimental to long-term success and may even reinforce your fears and anxieties in relation to leaving your comfort zone.

- Physical and mental preparation is key. Invest in this process and mentally acknowledge the sacrifice, giving yourself the very best chance of success.

- Temporary and incremental exposure to difficult activities, and learning to find the resolve to come through them, makes the rest of your life easier. Such exposures can include but are not limited to high-intensity training, controlled (safe) cold water exposure and working on academic or physical weaknesses, all of which afford an opportunity to encounter, endure and overcome adversity.

- Once the foundations of conditioning and the subsequent benefits of self-confidence are embedded, choose one physical activity – a high-intensity workout, for instance – and go all out. In doing so, learn how to manage and regulate your emotions during intense fatigue and challenging times. The body has an uncanny ability to send alarm signals (negative self-talk) wanting the mind to stop movement. Mental conditioning (practice) enables you to resist the temptation to succumb to these alarm bells, allowing you to break through the pain barrier and unlock greater personal capabilities.

- One's complement of self-discipline is the epitome of one's degree of self-control. Being able to say yes and no to the right things at the right time is essential. But conversely, we must differentiate between the inner voice that is trying to protect us to the detriment of progress. Therefore, we must learn which signals to act on and which to override during times of adversity.

- Emotional regulation and controlling how you react is one of the most self-empowering things you can develop.

CHAPTER FIVE

Phase Two: The Anti-Climax of Success

It was after the publication of *Becoming the 0.1%* that I realised that nothing I have ever accomplished has fully lived up to my expectations. Speaking modestly, this is a trait shared by other highly driven and successful people.[1] Arguably, the self-imposed high expectations placed on goal acquisition, underpinned by 'detrimental optimism' – a yearning for enduring happiness and fulfilment – have often been in dire conflict with the reality of achieving that aim.

Yes, I have experienced the euphoria we can all envision at certain positions of career privilege, but sadly, it has never lasted long – sometimes only a matter of days, or weeks at a push. Nonetheless, you would think that completing training and becoming a Royal Marines Commando would produce a euphoria that lasted for longer than that.

Upon leaving CTCRM, I was drafted to Fleet Protection Group Royal Marines (FPGRM, now renamed 43 Commando), a unit of around 500 Royal Marines in Scotland that mainly protected the UK's nuclear weapons deterrent, submarines, nuclear weapons and their arming bays, during a constant state of readiness. I had been told to avoid this posting by my

Training Team due to the main requirement of our presence there being a need to go 'behind the wire', as it was called. A tedious and soul-destroying existence confined to one of three maximum-security and highly secretive facilities for five weeks at a time.

Although this mundane reality was known to me, I eventually landed one of the best jobs in the Royal Marines. It was a specialist role within FPGRM, which was being assigned to Fleet Standby Rifle Troop (FSRT) as a 'Non-compliant Boarding Operator', a role handed down from the Special Boat Service (SBS). Operating in small specialist teams of six, we would deploy worldwide, boarding vessels against the crew's will or without their permission to disrupt weapons and narcotics smuggling and to counter piracy operations. What is more, we were also in a constant state of readiness for any humanitarian aid disaster, such as the Thailand tsunami in 2011.

Yet despite achieving my aim within the first six months, I had already started to encounter career disillusionment. In fact, glimmers of reality had begun emerging towards the end of training,[2] uncomfortable moments of realisation that the job would not live up to my expectations and it was not going to be worth the sacrifice.

Commando unit life

When I left Commando Training Centre and subsequently joined my new Commando unit, there were entrenched cultural norms at play that increased my disillusionment and further compounded the anti-climax.

First was the disparity between how I thought life would be post-training and the reality as a freshly trained Royal Marines

Commando. Deemed 'fresh out the box' (*out of training*), I found the first six months incredibly uncomfortable. What followed was an intensive integration process, a rite of passage that all 'new' Royal Marines had to go through.

I turned up at FPGRM nervous yet excited about what was in store. I was made fully aware of the dreaded 'Joining Runs' (*the initiation process*), where the lads would get the 'Fucking New Blokes' (FNBs) or 'Sprogs' as they called us and subject them to a process of often horrendous initiation practices in order to gain rightful passage into the troop. It was a hugely degrading process that brought you crashing right back down to earth after being in Kings Squad, the name given to the men who had completed all the training requirements and testing prior to leaving CTCRM, and literally thinking you could walk on water.

On my very first day in camp, my first detail was to go and see the Admin Sergeant in Gibraltar Building, basically the Marines HQ. This bloke would assign me to a troop. On my way from the grots (*accommodation*), I received a huge reality check. I was standing with another new Marine outside the camp shop with our hands in our pockets when we were stopped and made to stand briskly to attention by a Royal Marines sergeant. He said aggressively, 'Who the f*** do you two c**ts think you are, f****** new blokes cutting round here with your f****** hands in your pockets?'

I was utterly shocked that this was how you were spoken to once you had passed out of training. It was a massive wake-up call for me. It was clear from that very first interaction that we were not special at all, and it made me feel pretty damn low about things. I had not expected to be spoken to like that while wearing the Green Beret.

The only way to describe the environment during the initial stages of life as a 'trained Marine' is that it was like going to a new school and desperately trying to be liked by the cool gang, treading on eggshells with every word spoken in an attempt to safeguard yourself from being bullied. It was truly awful. Then came the news I had been dreading – a joining run was being planned for around six to eight of us.

Initiation

According to the lads, the joining run would take place behind the wire and preparation was well under way. Each day, thirty bored Royal Marines would think of every conceivable way possible to give the new lads the most horrendous evening of their young careers. If I am honest, I was absolutely dreading it and I would not make eye contact with any of the key troop instigators, who were senior ranks and alpha male in demeanour. In some ways, it was quite childlike. I genuinely thought that if I did not look at the lads organising the joining run during the lead-up or engage them in conversation, they would not notice me. I was filled with trepidation. I did not want to hear anything about it and every time it was mentioned, I felt a deep rush of adrenaline flood my body.

The night finally arrived. Six of us were due to take part, all of whom had completed training within the past three to six months. Leftover food had been collected over three days, then divided and put into six old grey school trays: the type where kids keep their books, course work, pens and pencils. The trays were accompanied by six empty buckets and six massive lines of pure chilli powder, and the door to the dreaded 'Hurt Locker' was open.

Now, the Hurt Locker was quite literally a locker big enough to fit one man without enough space to breathe in and out without his sternum touching the side panel. To enter it, the unfortunate bloke had to shimmy in sideways and he was ordered to stay in there until further notice without complaining or verbalising any sign of emotion. Occasionally, the lads would bang hard on the locker or even get around it and lay it on the floor, door down – so you couldn't get out if you tried. It was absolutely horrendous, but hilarious to witness.

First up was the three days' worth of leftovers and your performance here would determine how the rest of your night would go. The leftovers were breakfast, lunch and evening meals from thirty Marines, divided into six portions. They were piled high in the trays mentioned above. At the sound of 'Go!', you had to consume the contents as if your life depended on it, against a timer. Once sick, which you almost certainly were within a matter of seconds, you had to throw up into the bucket by your side and carry on until your tray was empty. This took up to two hours.

The winner was the one who had smashed his way through the tray of rotting food, or at the very least eaten the most first. They received a bye from the next events and earned respect from the lads. The losers had to drink their own sick, again within a time limit. As before, the winner drinking the most or finishing received a bye.

The four losers now had to compete at killer pool. For every missed pot, a line of pure chilli powder had to be snorted with zero reaction or emotion. The powder was so strong it carried a health warning on the back of the bottle that stated in black text and yellow background: *Use sparingly, high amounts can seriously damage your health and large quantities may even kill you.*

This got dark rather quickly from a sadistic point of view and at times it was almost impossible even to see the balls on the table (yes, I was still in the running) as our noses and eyes were pouring with water and red snot. The winners, who were myself and one other, received a bye from the next round. This left two lads remaining, who had to go into the Hurt Locker one at a time and basically endure it the longest. This was the ultimate endurance test. Lads would even set their alarms and wake up during the night at each hour just to bang and rattle on the locker to keep the guy awake. It was brutal.

Subsequently, even after our joining run, I found it hard to integrate fully and relax among my peers, with myself and the new lads constantly having to make wets (*drinks*) and getting detailed off on the less desirable little errands. Nevertheless, I was slowly gaining respect and building friendships

You are probably thinking, why the need for this initiation? It was about establishing absolute authority. At CTCRM, Royal Marines recruits who have moved onto the Commando phase naturally develop a perceived sense of seniority among the recruits in the lower stages of training. The junior and less senior recruits look at you in sheer awe, which makes you feel on top of the world.

Upon leaving CTCRM and going to your unit, however, the trained Marines already residing there, many of whom may have been on live operations, will quickly put the new lads back in their place. In short, you go from being the top dog at CTCRM to the 'Wets Bitch' (*tea and coffee maker*) at your new unit. It is such an intimidating experience, where the power balance flips significantly in favour of your new troop members.

Initiation for this purpose is to show the new recruits who is in charge, to remind them to follow orders without hesitation, and to enforce the strict social hierarchy within the Royal Marines.[3] Personally, I never deemed this part of the integration process necessary. I thought the rite of passage should have been assured based on one's ability to come through training and receive the Green Beret. Therefore, I found the whole initiation process and the first six months of life post-training to be degrading and detrimental to what had been a truly unbelievable accomplishment.

Training with the US Marines

During my time at FPGRM (Fleet Protection Group Royal Marines), we did a training exchange with the US Marines FAST company. The plan was for them to come over to the UK for a three-week training package in Scotland, followed by us going to Quantico, Virginia, in the USA.

The UK training package consisted of mountain training in Scotland on Ben Nevis, the Three Sisters and the Devil's Staircase in Glen Coe, with a field exercise thrown in for good measure at Garelochhead, a remote village on the west coast of Scotland. Shortly before the US Marines arrived, our Sergeant Major told us to wear our combat shirts with the sleeves rolled up. It was the middle of winter. He said, 'Trust me, fellas, they'll get off the bus in full warmers kit, take one look at you guys and it will break them instantly.' Unbelievably, at the end of the UK training exchange, that was the first thing their commander said to us: 'Gents, we kinda knew we were f***** the second we saw you guys wearing shirts!'

The US Marines had nowhere near our level of fitness and were not used to the weather or the terrain. They have so much money and so many military assets at their disposal, they admitted openly to us that they get either 'hummers' or 'choppers' to transport them everywhere, unlike the Royal Marines, who have to rely on good old-fashioned boots and physical and mental endurance.

We started on Ben Nevis, the UK's highest mountain, taking the back route not open to the public, which is often used by rock climbers and extreme mountaineers. At Check Point 1, the US Marines could no longer carry their kit: 50lbs plus weapon. So we were told we had to top flap – carry their kit plus ours all the way up – leaving them to climb and descend in clean fatigue (*no kit*). Astonishingly, even then some of the US Marines were crawling and complaining all the way – very embarrassing for an elite fighting force and a superpower nation. Their lame performance carried on to the following two mountains, which we completed in one day.

This trend continued into the field exercise. They just were not physically or mentally prepared for the three weeks' training with us, and to be perfectly honest, it was so 'jack' (selfish) of the Corps (*us*) to do that to them and expose them physically and mentally as we did. They were our guests and they learned absolutely nothing during their time with us, only that they were not at our level of physical fitness and mental robustness.

Basically, you can thrash anyone up and down mountains to some extent. It doesn't add to or pass on any technical or tactical soldiering skills. Cross-training should be about learning from each other – comparing ways of operating, sharing and reflecting on tactics and how to overcome complex problems during operations. On the contrary, they went home broken.

Three weeks later, it was our turn to visit the USA. The training package we received there was nothing short of outstanding.

We were taught how to fight effectively in CQB (close quarter battle) scenarios in large-scale, mock villages against the US Marines. It simulated fighting in urban environments, something the USMC (US Marine Corps) had become very accustomed to during the fierce fighting they experienced in Iraq, especially Fallujah. To make things more realistic, we used 'simunition' (*bullets with a paintball tip*) – not a nice experience if you were unlucky enough to get shot as they would often break the skin. This was without doubt the US Marine's bread and butter and their skills and tactical awareness in these settings were outstanding. They had us doing room clearances, complex building attacks and coordinated entrees.

During the early stages of the training, which was very intense, the US Marines were far better than us and kept gaining the upper hand during engagements. However, over the days that passed, we were learning fast. The final exercise was to attack and gain control of the entire village – three main areas that were under US Marine occupation. We did our rehearsals throughout the day and received our orders in the evening, with H hour (the time of day at which an attack, landing or other military operation is scheduled to begin) set for the early hours.

The plan was that three troops would simultaneously hit the three main buildings and outbuildings in the village complex, clearing them and taking control. At 2 a.m., we collectively and quietly walked into our positions under the cover of dense darkness. Thirty minutes later, all three teams of Royal Marines (with a major point to prove) stormed the three areas of the village, clearing it and taking control in fourteen minutes – faster than SWAT, Delta and SEAL Team 6 had done previously. The Americans were so dumbfounded by our tactics that they called our officers forward later to explain how we went about taking down the village.

We went onto the firing ranges next, where we had the full works of their latest weaponry and an endless supply of ammunition to go at, a proper 'Cowboy Range', as we call it in the Royal Marines – a lad's dream.

After the ranges came the USMC's payback for the 'seeing off' (foul play) they had received in Scotland. First, we had to do their Endurance Course, which is the course Clarice Starling is running during the opening scene of the film *The Silence of the Lambs*. The E-Course is a seven-mile assault course in full battle order (helmet, body armour and weapon) and is their version of our Endurance Course – needless to say, it was emotional, compounded by the fact that I had done no Phys for seven weeks. However, it was not a patch on our own Endurance Course, and that is not me being biased!

After that, we went straight onto their O-Course, their version of our Tarzan Assault Course. These two tests were planned and executed at the hottest point of the day in an effort to break us. However, two of our lads broke the all-time records on the two courses, which kind of backfired on the US Marines.

While in America, the USMC treated us to a weekend in Washington D.C., where we went to see the US Marine Corps Silent Drill Platoon, and this was nothing short of outstanding, totally breathtaking in fact. They throw their rifles with fixed bayonets up and over their shoulders with elaborate spins and tosses for others to catch in complete silence. Everything from their weapon movements to their synchronisation was performed and executed with absolute precision and their timing was impeccable.

In all, the experience in America was one of the highlights of my short career and to this day, one of the best things I have ever done in my life was fighting in those mock villages and interacting with the US Marines. It really was an eye-opener into the workings of the US military and highlighted the super-power they truly are, with no expense spared.

Reflecting deeper, this period emphasised the importance of bilateral cross-training and the fundamental need to park one's ego and perceived capability at the door. We operate in a very different way to the US military, and it was short-sighted to assume they needed to conform to earn our respect. In their own right they were exceptional and, in contemporary warfare, they were undoubtedly more tactically skilled and capable in urban settings.

What is more, such arrogance portrayed by us ultimately inhibited our ability to absorb such lessons from them; especially during the first three weeks they joined us in Scotland. You should always be open to learning from other people's experiences while possessing the cognitive flexibility to appraise situations from another's perspective.

In Scotland we wanted to prove our mental and physical superiority to the US Marines, when the whole point of the training exercise was for them to learn from our specialised expertise in unfamiliar terrain. In this example, we were thinking only about ourselves and not working together with our allies – or in the case of a business, our work associates – for the greater benefit of each other.

Stagnation, a lack of funding and imagination

What further compounded the anti-climax of success with the Royal Marines, inviting disillusionment, was a lack of personal development opportunities and continual training. Post CTCRM, I possessed a furious hunger to maximise my skills as an elite soldier, yet my efforts fell on deaf ears. Back then, all the good courses went to 'the boys' – friends of friends – the distribution of which was handed out by and to the senior ranks. Unbelievably, I was offered the courses I wanted only once I submitted my request to leave the Royal Marines, and by that time it was too late.

Our days were often spent watching daytime TV, the likes of *Trisha*, *Jeremy Kyle* and *Loose Women*, which was a cultural joke among the lads. Bizarrely, there were very few intense training packages and no real fundamental skills development once I left Commando Training Centre. It was astonishing and demotivating. The marketing to become a 'mystical' Royal Marines Commando – the adverts and the hysteria they drilled into us during training in 2005 – had made us all believe we would become super soldiers, engaged in unrestricted, elite operations around the world.

In reality, it was vastly different. I swiftly learned that those roles were undertaken by the Special Boat Service (SBS) or Special Air Service (SAS). In my opinion, we were massively underutilised. Subsequently, life as a trained Marine rarely made me feel special. The sense of achievement from completing training soon became a distance memory.

Post training, we were thrust into an environment where the Green Beret, something for which I had shed blood and tears, meant nothing. For those that had been out of the box a number of years, their Green Lids (*berets*) were simply part of their everyday uniform, like putting on a hard hat before entering a building site. It was not until you left the Royal Marine's bubble and entered other 'non' Royal Marines camps that you experienced the awe and respect awarded to what you had achieved, and during those rare occasions you wore the beret with a greater sense of pride.

As time passed, my attention turned to the money. I never joined the Royal Marines for the cash – I wanted to overcome the challenge. However, once that had been achieved and my grievances were cemented, I became increasingly aware of how little we were being paid. Back then I was on only £18,000 after one year of leaving CTC. A majority of senior ranks who had been in for a period of time often assured us how well the Corps looked after people, alluding to the dental and health-care packages among other quite insignificant benefits. But I never bought into it. I could see right through it and wanted to earn more money. In all honesty, I joined the Royal Marines to provide a solid platform, a stepping stone to pursue my ultimate desire of conducting 'private' hostile close protection operations in the likes of Iraq, Somalia or Afghanistan. So, in terms of the bigger picture, that was always on my radar.

Lesson 2

Mitigating the anti-climax of success

Studies have found that many high achievers are guilty of setting the bar too high on performance outcomes and often project forward irrationally, misjudging what the positive effects of achieving an aim will be and therefore underplaying the potentially negative impact on their mental wellbeing.[4]

I have had the pleasure of interviewing the rugby union player and Women's Rugby World Cup winner, Vicky Fleetwood (see Chapter 12: The Interviews) and during the interview, she said, 'When I accomplish something, it's always onto the next thing. Always has been!' This really struck a chord with me, as it was exactly what I would say facing the same questioning. So I asked Vicky, 'Do you ever feel accomplished at something? Have you ever felt a sense of fulfilment once you have reached a personal goal or career milestone, for example?

Can you say, that's enough now, I've arrived. I can chill and live off the back of that now?' She replied:

You think something will give you fulfilment but it never truly does. The journey being tough and the learnings you get are what you kind of strive for ... The biggest anti-climax for me was winning the World Cup with England. Obviously you get the exhilaration of winning, but the biggest [feeling] for me at the time was a sense of relief, like, I can finally breathe now, which shouldn't be your mindset upon winning such an incredible thing. We had a year building up to it, and it changed my life in lots of small ways, but then straight after, I was like, what's next?

Therefore, once a goal or milestone is accomplished, the ultimate challenge is often to avoid the subsequent dip in mental wellbeing. The realisation of a goal can mark the moment when a specific prescription of thinking and behaviour is no longer needed, thus inviting a natural opportunity to descend from optimal performance and mental wellbeing.

For example, during my studies at university, my mental health took a sharp dive once the study year had finished. More recently, on the day of publication of my first book, I remember feeling mixed emotions, but overwhelmingly, rather deflated – a sense of sadness that the journey had ended. In both instances, I experienced subsequent bouts of depression.

Although the job did not live up to my expectations and left me feeling extremely bitter for a number of years, there were some unforeseen benefits to staying on course and seeing the goal through to fruition. Finishing what I started two and a half years earlier, and withstanding the high attrition rates inherent in training, were absolutely crucial to nurturing my inner growth, maturity and personal development. What I did not realise back then was that I was gaining so much experience and self-understanding while on that journey, and that was invaluable.

Historically, most of my goal or career anti-climaxes were in part due to misplaced optimism, and through reflection I have come to realise that I like the chase – the journey towards goal acquisition – rather than reaching the finishing line. In fact, thinking about it, I have never celebrated any of my past achievements. Instead, I have immediately reset my sights on another challenge.

Therefore, reflecting on previous journeys towards achievements has allowed me to realise two crucial things: (a) when we are engaged in goal acquisition, we are growing, subtly getting better, engaged in a process of becoming more effective and more well rounded, and (b) we have purpose, and that is absolutely essential to being a human being.

Yes, the journey is often uncertain and littered with adversity and complexity, but the small wins you get when you overcome something, and ultimately remain on track, equip you with better personal understanding, and that is invaluable. It is the little wins that maintain the stimulus to continue and which make the journey so worthwhile. It is in these rich moments that we find the most fulfilment, where we feel the most joy and personal contentment.

Therefore, we should cherish the journey towards achievements and refrain from placing too much weight on finding happiness at the end because it is rare to find it there. Especially to the extent that we ultimately desire. It is not the achievement that changes us, it is the process towards it, and that is a beautiful thing (see Figure 5.1).

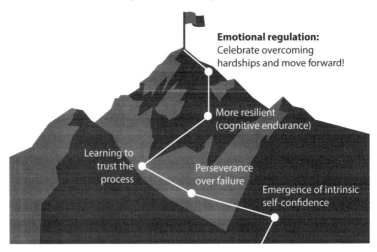

A Journey of Growth:
It's not just about reaching the summit…

Emotional regulation:
Celebrate overcoming
hardships and move forward!

More resilient
(cognitive endurance)

Learning to
trust the
process

Perseverance
over failure

Emergence of intrinsic
self-confidence

Figure 5.1 Personal growth is embedded in the journey, it is not waiting at the finishing line

PRACTICAL APPLICATIONS

- Anti-climaxes happen to all of us. Anticipating that this will happen to some degree allows us to take control and mitigate such outcomes. Therefore, learning to find comfort in and enjoy the journey while not putting too much mental weight on the end goal will soften the impact of anti-climaxes.

- Sometimes it is easy to become downbeat and disenchanted once we have arrived at a career milestone. Maybe, as in my case, it is not what we imagined it was going to be like. Nonetheless, see this as one piece of the jigsaw puzzle in relation to your whole life. Take a moment to acknowledge the bigger picture.

- See goal or career milestones as stepping stones. Thus, strategically place each milestone in order of importance and acknowledge that each one is merely a part of the overall journey. This will limit the tendency to place so much emotional energy on any one stepping stone.

- The journey *is* the personal development process – a period of time that cultivates self-confidence and growth via overcoming the arm-wrestle of complexity. Therefore, any exposure to it is always beneficial.

- Ultimately, we must acknowledge that once an endeavour or strategic life goal is accomplished, a prescription of thinking is no longer required due to a lack of stimulus dependency, therefore emotional wellbeing may plummet as we descend from optimal performance, regather and refocus.

- Anti-climaxes are part and parcel of the journey, just as failure is the underrated best friend of success.

CHAPTER SIX

Phase Three: Removing the Stimulus

After leaving the Royal Marines, I did not really have a back-up plan. I just needed to get out. I started working as a freelance personal trainer and worked part-time as a residential care support worker, looking after twelve- to sixteen-year-old kids who had sadly been placed in care. Both roles bored me to tears. They did not stimulate me in the slightest or provide the potentially fast, adrenaline-fuelled occupation I was still seeking. I suppose this short transitional phase taught me, yet again, what I did *not* want.

I needed a goal to aim for, a stimulus to focus my attention fully and lock me into a process of adventure and self-discovery; the alternative looked very grim and ordinary. So I decided to pursue my desire to land a role as a close protection operator (CPO) in the hostile private security sector, known as 'the circuit'.

One thing I did find interesting during this period was my perceived lack of self-worth. I felt lost and as if I had gone backwards. As if my identity was eroding in some way and I was back to being just average, even though I had desperately wanted to leave the Marines. In a strange way, being a Royal Marine had massaged my ego. It seemed to provide a stimulus in the sense of how I perceived myself and it forced me to conform in a subtle way. Being a Marine had made me feel purposeful, a part of something great, even if that was based on the reputation alone. Without the structure, quite frankly, I felt lost.

During this transitional period, it would have been easy to slip back into my old ways prior to joining the Marines. My local environment was devoid of opportunity and inspiration; it encapsulated a life of working to make ends meet and then spending the rest in the local pub. The thought of living that existence was so depressing, yet prolonged exposure to it pulled me back in. Once again, as if I had been thrust seven years back in time, my weekends were spent in the pub, drinking too much and occasionally taking drugs.

This is such an important distinction to make, but personal integrity and self-understanding is key. Maintaining behavioural alignment and focused intent towards our goals and long-term success is never straightforward. Detrimental behaviours and temporary derailments can and often do happen, especially when we are forced to conform for long periods to strict cultural norms, for example, or when applying strict self-discipline and resilience. It is, however, essential to acknowledge such triggers and personal occurrences and to regain goal-oriented consistency as soon as possible. Eventually, such behaviours will erode over time and new coping and attentional restoration methods will be established.

The power of the stimulus

Speaking personally, the revelation after leaving the Royal Marines is that the degree of self-assurance and mental resilience that I was able to harness to achieve success and become a Royal Marines Commando has never been fully realised again.

As I progressed from week one to week thirty-two in training, I was able to push myself through and beyond any pain barriers. I could operate with little to no sleep for days, I was not remotely fazed by living out in the field during severe weather conditions, I didn't feel distressed when the Training Team instantly shattered our morale.

Due to a period of mental conditioning to environmental demands, I found myself at the uppermost frontiers of what was possible mentally and physically. I became desensitised to the arduous and often traumatic regime of military training. But that ability was not long-lasting once it had been acquired. It was only a temporary adjustment upheld by the environment I inhabited at that time. Once I left and re-entered civilian life, I became mentally weaker: my negative self-talk increased (and I listened) and I was influenced more by others. I started to question my ability and my perception of myself.

It was during my time in the Royal Marines, that the 'demand stimulus' – the environment and the value attached to the end goal – elicited and crucially maintained my mindset. This produced the behavioural output that synced perfectly with aspirational alignment, inducing a rare form of desire underpinned by resilience. A cognitive endurance that was remarkably flexible and adaptable to change yet was ultimately geared towards the ferocious effort to achieve one outcome.

However, like the trajectory of a bullet, leaving the barrel with purpose and intent, I was naturally losing energy over the course of my flight, gradually dipping towards the ground in terms of my cognitive endurance and mental capacity. At the beginning, there is an energy 'window' of maximum velocity and potential impact.

Energy management and distribution

Envision any focused goal or aspirational period like manipulating an hourglass. When it is in the optimum vertical position, the hourglass allows the sand to cascade down rapidly and efficiently, in doing so discharging its load from the top chamber to the bottom. Its energy and output are high: it is efficient in terms of the time taken to achieve that aim, yet the resources in the top chamber are swiftly running empty, like our own minds. Unless the hourglass is turned laterally to slow down or lie at rest for a period, it will quickly run dry and have nothing left to give until it is turned upside down and allowed to reload. Our attentional resources are no different.

By analysing my experiences in relation to performance during the past eighteen years and from conversations with other fellow Royal Marines and successful athletes, I have found that we rarely engage such optimisation unless (a) we make it something deeply personal. But (b) when we do, I don't believe mindset can endure at optimum output without factoring in planned rest to bring attentional resources back closer to baseline. Failing to do so can result in cognitive depletion, opening the door to mental health issues. Put simply, we can maintain effective and prolonged connection to the stimulus for longer and arrive at the end in a better state, with more attuned understanding and energy management strategies.

On the one hand, if such an analogy is correct, it could explain the cognitive highs we experience in terms of progress and overcoming adversity. These are in part due to elements of positive reinforcement and endorphin release – the sense of elation and increased self-confidence we encounter by overcoming obstacles along the way – which maintain the desired behaviour. On the other hand, it could highlight the lows we experience in mood and self-worth when we encounter negative reinforcement from internal or external setbacks, or by removing the stimulus. If anything, by acknowledging the potential for instability in the construct of mindset, it allows us to understand its transient nature. This facilitates the propensity for an attentive 'energy management strategy,' such as factoring in a rest and recuperation framework around the maintenance of performance (see the next chapter), which is key.

But more so, it begins to highlight the dangers of the relentless pursuit of goal or career milestone acquisitions and the challenges a successful person must overcome to remain at the top of their chosen field.

I believe we get only a handful of focused and attuned 'mindset resilience windows' during our lives, where a stimulus – a personal goal or career milestone – harnesses the power within us to overcome anything. This stimulus will unlock the utmost capability of our minds during the process of goal acquisition, if we dare to commit to it by leaving our comfort zone.

However, what is left to uphold this level of elite behaviour once someone has reached their destination and the stimulus has come to an end? It can be very difficult to continue past a significant personal milestone with the same self-discipline and imposed sacrifice it took to arrive there. In keeping with the hourglass notion, if an individual arrives at a point of mental depletion, then as with all forms of organic energy, adequate time to rest and recharge is required, but this is often neglected. Often, no matter the costs, we quickly reload with an 'empty' magazine and try to go again without adequate rest and attentional restoration.

The subjectivity of our mental state at any given time and a lack of understanding are to blame, making falling off the rails ever more likely. But there is something else . . . we fail to maintain the stimulus and thus our behaviour. For example, have you ever been successful with a dieting plan to meet your goal of the ideal physique? Perhaps this was for a holiday or a wedding, or simply to make you feel better. Once the target has been reached, we have a systemic tendency to fall off the wagon and crash. Due to a lack of long-term planning and the effective implementation of lifestyle habits – call it balance – we return to the softer options that facilitate weight gain, such as a lack of consistency in the gym or in exercise, or not thinking about calorie consumption and thus gorging on fast foods. The same happens to all successful people, regardless of their occupation, highlighting the fragility of mindset when self-discipline is not upheld or required by the stimulus.

Training-induced bipolar

Consider this. At the summit of one's mental optimisation, without proper maintenance what if the only way left to go is down? What if, organically, we start descending from optimal performance and mental health stability once we have achieved our personal goals? After all, what is left afterwards in terms of resolve? We never appear to acknowledge the fragility of mental resilience or its limitations, and what maintains self-discipline once the stimulus is removed.

For example, could the depression that follows an achievement be due to mental or physical fatigue? As mentioned above, any form of concentrated energy must require rest and recovery at some stage. Psychologically, if the journey travelled releases endorphins on the way up, creating a high while absorbing attentional resources, then it is obvious to assume that our mood must take a hit as our system rebalances itself.

In 2023, I spoke to Dr Stuart Wilkinson, the former Leeds Rhinos, England rugby league and Great British Lions assistant coach. Stuart had also just completed a PhD in High Performance Leadership. We discussed this phenomenon regarding the highs and lows experienced by sports professionals and athletes and he alluded to their daily training life. For instance, the need to keep switching energy and focus on and off during a player's or athlete's daily programming when building up to a game, maintaining performance or a goal.

Once the day is finished or the season over – maybe even when someone's career is finally over – these emotional ups and downs over the years can result in a vulnerability to mental illness. Although we both acknowledge a lack of available research in this area, Stuart calls this effect 'training-induced bipolar'. To counter the emergence of such issues, elite rugby league clubs with which he has been involved have introduced a 'point system on lifestyle away from training programme'. This system maps data on the player's mental health and wellbeing away from the team environment. Stuart stressed that focusing on player welfare away from the 'office' and looking at the bigger picture was essential to maintaining performance through behavioural alignment.

Another thing to consider is: what if people simply fall out of love with what they are doing? I appreciate this is often difficult to comprehend, especially when someone occupies a desired role or position of privilege. But look at it this way, every material object we acquire during our lifetime loses its value at some point and a goal or career milestone is no different.

The stimulus upholds and harnesses the power to elicit an obsessive behavioural attachment and massages our contentment and satisfaction for a period, but for most people, its effects will slowly decrease. Much like the potency of a hypothetical love potion, upon first consumption the chemical reaction is strong, but as time passes it will gradually wear off. What is attractive and treasured on one day becomes less desirable in the succeeding days, as the flaws and negatives slowly become apparent, for example when we understand how much a new car is costing per month after the initial honeymoon period. The exact same thing happens with positions of privilege. We get bored.

In this notion, we take for granted anything we acquire or accomplish after a period; the facade crumbles away as we see more of the reality that lies behind the curtains. It is during this period that the stimulus becomes less potent and behavioural alignment becomes compromised. This opens up a whole host of potentially damaging factors to the underpinnings of sustained performance outcomes such as second-phase goal acquisition and the maintenance of our mental health.

To look at this another way, an interest or passion rarely engages us for life. They come and go with ageing. You have only to look at the phases of interest during childhood – dolls, train sets and action figures, for example – compared to the trends and pastimes that we get into during our adult lives. Very few people hold a passion for something during a whole lifetime. Therefore, mental flexibility is key – in all facets – to migrate change and life transitions successfully.

Lesson 3

Learning to thrive in transition; maintaining strategic behaviour
Before we explore this lesson, it is important to acknowledge two fundamentals in terms of behavioural alignment and goal acquisition:

- First, no goal is achievable without the implementation of 'consistent' routines.

- Second, inconsistent self-discipline and a lack of investment to maintain or adjust 'positive' daily routines compromises behavioural and goal alignment, resulting in disorderly daily mismanagement and thus a lack of strategic control.

Establishing routines, then, lays the foundation for successful outcomes and provides the building blocks for someone to thrive in dynamic circumstances. To highlight the need for establishing routine in transition, I am going to draw upon an extreme example to illustrate the strategic value that can be harnessed in adverse settings to promote one's ability to thrive when going to and from new environments.

CAMP LIFE DEMANDS

If they are to realise success on the 32-week-long course, Royal Marines recruits must negotiate the rigours of elite military training via a constant need to transition (and thrive) in two equally arduous yet contrasting environments.

Life on camp is defined by intensive time pressure, therefore recruits must learn to adapt to the ever-changing and increasing daily schedule, which is broken into periods of learning and physical exercise. To navigate the demands of each day successfully requires thorough preparation, applied consistently and upheld by self-discipline, and this is attained by the systematic preparation invested during the previous day. Due to the intensive nature of the daily schedule, there is simply no time to carry out personal administration on the day. Therefore, failure to prepare results in recruits falling quickly behind the learning curve and if left unchecked will eventually result in failing the course.

FIELD LIFE DEMANDS

Life in the field also brings the same time and commitment pressures; however, basic life support is non-existent. Field exercises are incredibly tough and require a vast amount of personal resolve and self-discipline. Recruits inhabit the field to learn how to survive and acquire the key specialist tactical skills at individual, section and troop level, in locations such as Woodbury Common, Dartmoor or Salisbury Plain. Such environments require the immediate implementation of routine in order to facilitate the foundation for coping mentally in such places, but crucially, the ability to thrive and thus lay a solid platform to conduct strategic behaviour.

In the initial phase, recruits are taught to establish basic living conditions: to make shelter, prepare food and initiate a routine of personal administration – cleaning their kit, maintaining good foot health, cleaning weapons and familiarising themselves with the immediate area. All this creates control and comfort in new surroundings and it establishes a baseline level for 'self-preserving human needs' and thus successful outcomes: the ability to thrive in any environment.

DAY-TO-DAY LIFE DEMANDS

Our daily commitments are no different and can demand the same complexity. Therefore the same approach to establishing routine is vital and should not be overlooked. Such tasks include making food for the following day, ensuring that previous day behaviours facilitate an early morning start to make the gym before work, and getting to work on time, as well as preparing content for meetings, completing other work-related tasks and juggling the demands of our personal lives. The quality of routines and the self-discipline applied to maintain them will determine the degree of success one will encounter.

A LACK OF ROUTINE DURING TRANSITION

A lack of foresight, planning and mental preparation hinders successful transitions. 'Acceptance' plays a key role here, as with the examples above, when sometimes we move into a new phase of life that does not provide the same familiarity or comforts as the one we have just left. When changing careers, for instance, or a relationship breaks down, or perhaps we are learning to adapt to the new demands of an injury or illness. Paris Fury, the wife of heavyweight boxing champion Tyson Fury, once revealed, 'Tyson's mental health dips dramatically when he doesn't have a routine or a schedule [a stimulus or purpose].'[1]

In my experience, every potential negative or complex life transition, or unavoidable change, embodies the following emotional process that we must overcome: Denial > Anger > Bargaining > Depression > Acceptance.[2]

- The first four stages put the mind in a past reality = distracted/ineffective.

- Acceptance places mind and body in the present reality = 'cognitive flexibility', able to adapt and react to change and crucially maintain performance.

For me, acceptance is the key construct of mental resilience. The ability to accept adversity and change quickly is essential if one is to thrive in the present, remain attentive and uphold performance. Dwelling on the past – what was or could have been – makes an individual ineffective in the present. Arriving at acceptance, however, is a skill that must be practised during the initial realisation of grief, disappointment or adversity, when something has not gone the way you expected.

During Marines training, the Training Team would come into the accommodation block during the early hours unannounced. One day they told us to get everything we owned, including our bedding, and throw it all out of the window on a cold and wet winter morning. Waking up to this reality is incredibly tough, as it means from that moment on you are up all night, undertaking their wishes and then washing, ironing and turning round your locker and living space ready for inspection the following morning.

In terms of mitigating the transition from what has been and gone to the reality you are now living in, look at it this way: nothing is going to change in the initial moment. Denial does not help, anger is a pointless emotion and must be controlled, and bargaining ... well, when have you ever been able to bargain with the orders of a sporting referee? Once a decision is made, it is final.

Then there is depression. Now situational depression, induced by poor lifestyle choices such as poor planning or drinking excessive amounts of alcohol, is very different from chronic depression. Situational depression can be controlled and averted with an analysis of the bigger picture and better lifestyle choices, which allows one to arrive swiftly at acceptance. Acknowledging the emotional process we embark on when faced with grief or adversity enables us to speed up the journey to acceptance, which is where we are most effective. After all, that is where we end up over time, so why not make the effort to get there sooner?

Therefore, the first four stages are a distraction, however real the emotional burden can feel. They are a hindrance to one's ability to remain in the present and in control, thus able to maximise effectiveness on the new environmental demands to maintain performance.

The power of acceptance, then, allows one to gain mental (internal) control immediately in often uncontrollable (external) situations. Acceptance provides the cognitive bridge during adversity that facilitates the transfer of strategic behaviour if the stimulus is damaged or removed, which is especially vital to prepare the mind for goal, career or end-of-career transitional adversity.

Planning for transitional change or potential goal-related obstacles is crucial to facilitate effective progression and to maximise performance, thus maintaining the emotional regulation of our mental health from one situation to the next. Foresight and planning, via the implementation of flexible yet strategic routines, are essential if we are to uphold behavioural alignment.

The taboo of depression and mental health issues in successful people

In 2022, Sir Bradley Wiggins spoke about his mental health battles. During a Talking Heads interview with *Men's Health*, he cited a lack of daily routine as being a major contributor to his onset of depression. Wiggins claimed that after winning the Tour de France, he stopped enjoying cycling and found himself trying to win for other people. His depression was perhaps compounded further by the subsequent realisation and possible anti-climax of reaching his ultimate end goal (winning the Tour de France), followed by the removal of the stimulus (entering into retirement).

This could be argued to be a taboo revelation, given that Wiggins competed in one of the toughest sports in the world, professional cycling – one that is underpinned by mental toughness, insular resolve and resilience. But it shows how fluid mindset and mental states can be and how they are dependent upon environment and a stimulus. It also highlights the importance of routine and structure, not only for eliciting performance but in regulating mental health and wellbeing: one's sense of self.

Jamie Peacock MBE, the former GB Lions and England rugby league captain, realised that it was time to retire when he started to lose his motivation:

The last year I played I had gotten really fed up with things. I found it hard to maintain my standards. To motivate myself, I kept reiterating to myself that this year would probably define me. So I decided to set a standard on my performances for how people would remember me. I went out on my terms. That's what I wanted to do – to go out on top!

I was never good at rugby as a kid. I was someone who played rugby, but I wasn't a rugby player. Rugby didn't define my identity, if you get me? Acceptance at the end was key in allowing me to move on, not dwell on what had been and gone. This helped me to fully shut the door.

People struggle with retirement or big transitions because they don't have an acceptance. When I looked in the mirror [at the end of his career], I didn't see a rugby player anymore, I just saw someone who once played rugby. I saw it as a part of my story – and that's a small yet big distinction. Also, expressing gratitude for the career I had, [that] really helped me to move on.

Such a life-changing withdrawal from professional competition is often inherently devoid of routine and purpose. To support the humanistic requirement to establish routine from a psychological perspective, we must look at Abraham Maslow's Hierarchical Theory of Human Needs (Figure 6.1).[3] This argues that human beings must establish their self-preserving (survival) needs before they can effectively move up the strategic hierarchy to achieve success and thrive in any environment. A lack of daily routine not only inhibits success, it also catastrophically affects the internalisation of one's purpose for those who have previously lived a life 'kept on the rails' by a stimulus or goal.

The swift and sudden removal of one's cultural environment, such as a professional team structure, can be massive for retiring or transitioning professional athletes. For example, when I chatted to Vicky Fleetwood in 2023, she felt a massive void in her life after retiring from her successful career in women's rugby union. She filled it by jumping into the sport

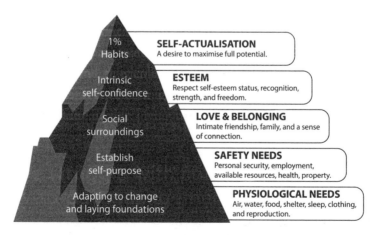

Figure 6.1 Maslow's Pyramid of Hierarchical Needs amended (right) with performance behaviours and potential outcomes (left)

of CrossFit, where she was surrounded by like-minded people once again. She said this was fundamental to maintaining her mental health and sense of belonging.

The analysis

What these cases demonstrate is the propensity for fragility among those whom we consider to have 'elite mindsets', a possible consequence of being engaged in high-level programmes or pursuing prolonged complex goals. The point is that these people have had to develop a certain mindset – an elite, finely tuned way of thinking and behaviour that is in direct alignment with their chosen profession – not only to reach the top and turn professional but to become the elite among elite athletes. Conversely, such behavioural alignment is not always transferable and thus in line with life and the demands away from the office.

PRACTICAL APPLICATIONS

- The self-discipline that underpins the growth mindset and facilitates behavioural output and alignment cannot survive without the stimulus that uniquely captures the individual. In that sense, mindset is extremely fragile.

- Our lives are defined by transitions and how we navigate such changes will define us.

- Robust routines are the basis of behavioural alignment – paradoxically, while they facilitate self-discipline, they need consistent self-discipline to survive.

- Arriving at acceptance is essential if we are to remain effective in the present. The four previous stages of the grief model keep us distracted and in the past.

- Learning to accept quickly is not easy – it must become a practised path upon experiencing adversity. Understanding the series of such negative emotions in the face of adversity helps to remind us that we must speed up the process to acceptance. It is a skill.

- In life, those who can adapt and accept change quickly, while re-establishing strategic routines in contrasting environments the fastest, will thrive in any situation and ultimately become the most successful over time.

- Discipline leads to Habits > Habits lead to Consistency > Consistency leads to Growth.

- Finally, to uphold self-discipline, you must keep the stimulus alive.

CHAPTER SEVEN

Phase Four: Maintaining Behavioural Alignment

The ability to maintain behavioural alignment over a sustained period is an extremely complex undertaking. However, at its heart must lie the crucial acknowledgement and weaponisation of consistency as a fundamental foundation. Personally, I have never struggled with staying consistent with my behavioural and goal alignment once I have committed fully to achieving, or at least trying to reach, an aim, but it has always taken its toll. The trade-off has been damage to my mental wellbeing.

Maintaining performance requires the mental flexibility to adapt to daily changes that threaten aspirational derailment and the resilience to withstand the mundane nature of 'progressional investment'. At the same time, it is necessary to mitigate the emotional rollercoaster of performance regressions and the disillusionment that follows when motivation subsides.

Look, upholding the consistency to safeguard behavioural alignment can be a gruelling process, especially in the face of fatigue and adversity. But with concerted practice, executing success behaviours, like going for a run even when tired and fatigued, we begin to establish innate behavioural responses, which are often underpinned by guilt and the anxiety of regression.

Such responses are 'success allies,' which kick in like a fail safe when motivation or desire depart. Like the power of acceptance, they prevent self-loathing, enabling the seamless transition of performance and reducing any tendency to welcome comfort when we feel particularly vulnerable.

That is why it is essential to note that when it comes to performance and progression, we cannot expect to keep getting better day in and day out . . . and when we don't, instantly throw in the towel.

Introducing 'healthy consistency'

Consistent performance is not about steadily getting better but about regularly turning up – being in the fight, despite setbacks, falls in performance or self-confidence, at an individual or collective level – while dealing with life's external challenges.

In any given moment, all someone can do is execute directed action towards a goal-oriented responsibility with as much perfection as possible, based on their current energy level or mental state. The constant repetition of this behavioural response will become subconscious action (*innate behaviour*) and that sparks the art of mastering healthy consistency. It is about being there, in the fight, even if sometimes that is just going through the motions. In this notion, consistency should be viewed from a marathon runner's rather than a sprinter's perspective – preserving cognitive resources through emotional composure – remaining patient and staying composed, if at times you are temporarily overtaken.

Workouts Rated

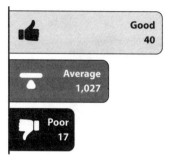

Figure 7.1 Three years of a world-class athlete rating their performance

Check out Figure 7.1. This shows three years of a world-class athlete rating every single workout as poor, average or good. As you can see, average data dominated. Good or great workouts are rare and constantly searching for them only invites disappointment and unnecessary disillusionment. Success is *not* determined by a great day. It comes from stacking month after month of solid days. Consistency compounds. Or put another way: being 80 per cent for 100 per cent of the time is better than being 100 per cent for 50 per cent of the time. That is healthy consistency.

The power of the one-percenters

Figure 7.2 provides a visible representation of outcome when doing nothing at all in terms of personal development vs making small, 1 per cent consistent extra efforts over twelve months: $(1.00)365 = 1.00$ vs $(1.01)365 = 37.00$.

So what exactly are the 1 per cent daily efforts? They are the attentions to detail we perform daily that are solely goal

The Daily Investment Rule

1% Daily Commitment
- Builds momentum
- Establishes positive habits
- Encourages a positive mindset
- Cultivates discipline and resilience
- Creates a foundation for success
- Enhances skills with consistent practice

No Daily Commitment
- Lacks discipline
- Prolongs negative habits
- No growth or improvement
- Greater vulnerability to setbacks
- Skills remain stagnant or decline
- Potential for unfulfillment and regret

Figure 7.2 No daily commitment vs 1 per cent daily commitment

oriented. Much like Ericsson's violinists (see Chapter Two), when systemic forward planning informs attention to detail through behavioural enactment, the disparity in results can be devastating in terms of trajectory and performance outcomes.

The one-percenters, a term commonly used in the world of sport and elite military organisations, are almost like a calling, a collective yet individual responsibility to maximise and harness every single aspect of the ingredients needed to cultivate and elicit the elite edge of performance.

Applications in non-elite settings: our everyday environments

The self-discipline to adhere to the principles of attention to detail, and the consistent application of such behaviours, are what produce the elite among elite performance outcomes.

In our everyday life, it could be the daily investment in our personal weaknesses in relation to our careers, through the application of deliberate practice, such as gaining more work-related knowledge through courses or reading specific self-help literature. It might be nurturing new skills or working on our personal passions, maybe exploring an entrepreneurial inclination or developing side projects. In short, it is a conviction to get better by exhausting any possible advantage or angle and then investing – no matter how small or deemed insignificant – to give you an edge in performance or success. When peeled back, it is the manner in which you create and live life – a lifestyle dedicated to success utilising the instruments of body and mind. It is about being strategic with the respective downtime that we all have in our daily lives and choosing how to use that effectively.

Do you finish work and sign off completely, or do you subscribe to the one-percenters and sacrifice an hour or two of relaxation, declining social invitations and engagements to put in the work? You maintain momentum in strategic, success-related behaviours by not drinking and by prioritising sleep to maximise the opportunities the following day. For example, by not viewing time off (on evenings and weekends) as being strictly time off. This is where the edge is and where, over a period of time, you begin to pull away.

A crucial 1 per cent behaviour is the timely management of sleep.[1] An hour of sleep before midnight is worth two after[2] because our internal biological clock sends signals to the brain to prepare the body for sleep. Therefore, by adhering to good patterns of sleep hygiene, we set ourselves up for maximum impact and productivity the following day. Time spent awake post-midnight goes against the harmony of our biological system[3] and is thus detrimental to performance.

Another 1 per cent behaviour could be a non-negotiable intention to exercise regularly in order to improve mental toughness and physical aesthetics through a structured programme. This also boosts wellbeing regulation through the production of endorphins, which has been proven to enhance mood and productivity:[4] benefits that promote better sleep, weight control and intimate family and social relationships.[5]

It is also vital to eat a good and balanced diet to give your body and mind the very best nutrition and fuel. If sports-related, you could be doing specific, performance-related extras such as explosive sprint work, strength and power resistance work, body and mind conditioning, or progressive cardio-based workouts. You could use sports-specific or recovery-based massages or physiotherapy, if necessary, coupled with nutritional advice to add, lose or maintain weight.

Subscribing to the benefits of attention to detail and implementing the healthy application of consistency to uphold such behaviours is where the elite edge of performance resides in the one-percenters. Fundamentally, it is how you conduct your life *in* but more so *away* from the 'office'. When it comes to aspiration, many leave their commitments to personal career goals on their desk at the close of business, thinking their work is done. Others simply go through the motions, with their mind transfixed on the coming evening or weekend, not realising that large parts of their lives are not being utilised effectively. Meanwhile, a small amount of personal development investment could be having a huge impact on their opportunities and earning potential in the years to come.

Look, I get it, work is work – we don't always like it and often would opt not to do it – we want to have a life away from work. The thing is that you will always be a slave to the system unless you develop your game away from the office. Make yourself different, unique and not beholden to your employer. That is power.

Just imagine if you left the office and worked on your own projects or aspects of personal development across the areas where you felt weak. If your life away from the office was constructed strategically to nurture successful, performance-based outcomes. Look again at Figure 7.2 and acknowledge how much value can be amassed over the course of one year, with *just* 1 per cent of strategic performance-based behavioural output invested.

Let me tell you something: that resonates in all aspects of life – it provides the edge no one else can see, attain or compete with.

The colouring book example

When it comes to outcome vs input vs approach, I want you to imagine stumbling across a complex colouring book for older children or adults.

The book has complex pictures divided into very small, technical sections. Now, literally anyone can take a crayon or felt tip and colour it in – misusing the colours in certain places, not shading in properly and carelessly crossing the lines into other sections. However, the whole picture will look a mess. Yes, it is coloured in, but not with care, intent and, most importantly, precision.

Whereas someone could acquire all the correct tools: the full complement of colour variations required and a selection of felt tips, from thick to fine. Once set up, they proceed to colour in and do so with dedicated focus and a commitment not to breach the lines.

Of course, this process takes longer. It is more painstaking and may take a few sittings to finish the full piece, but what you are left with is a feast of vibrant colour and a general outcome of perfection.

> The input needed was arguably the same: all one
> had to do was colour in the picture. But the approach
> to the task created two completely different outcomes.
> That is the power of attention to detail.

When I talked to Dr Stuart Wilkinson, the former England and Great Britain rugby league assistant coach, he told me that maintaining performance is all about developing habits and rituals that become embedded in an individual's or team's psychology. These are nurtured through good team and organisational cultures, which are made possible through clever programming.

Maintaining performance needs to become innate and one's ability to self-regulate is absolutely fundamental to success as a professional player, but also for the team. For example, players can learn how to control their emotions during high-pressure stakes by practising composure before and during game play and holding onto their self-control during periods of adversity – both on and off the field.

In terms of maintaining behavioural alignment as a team, Dr Stuart talked about the process of losing and how players need to revisit the trauma of personal mistakes or losing big games through a clearly devised process of debriefing, known as 'post event reflection'. That means addressing the positives and negatives: what went right and what lessons can be learned from an individual or team perspective moving forward. This is then implemented during the following week of training. In terms of maintaining performance via momentum, he stressed the need to have a clearly devised Plan B, C and so on. This would prepare the team for adversity and arm them with the mental flexibility to adapt quickly.

When it came to player discipline or certain players not fully conforming to their professional standards, a player could arrive on game day to be told they were the eighteenth man. Basically, not selected to play, but in the squad in case of illness prior to the game starting. From personal experience, this is a truly awful position to be in, but as Dr Stuart argued, it establishes authority.

More importantly, it also serves to elicit a response in the player. Upon hearing you are the eighteenth man, how do you respond on game day? Do you help and assist the team and coaching staff, or do you sulk and harbour resentment? For me, this is a process of acceptance, one of many situations in which a player must learn to self-regulate.

In order to safeguard continual effort to sustain performance and alignment, Dr Stuart introduced a 'rapid appraisal system' on performance and quality statistics. Through experience, he had found greater levels of success in coaching players and producing results not by adding value on all the 'fancy plays' – scoring goals or tries, for example – but in adding value on 'effort plays', such as try-saving tackles, carries, loose-ball recovery efforts and defensive effort communication.

For the player, whenever the less fancy, often less acknowledged, efforts were executed, they were scored on a points basis and then added to the team's, but more importantly, the player's, stats. During game review post-match, this system was proven to encourage individual and thus collective team efforts in all aspects of game play, which resulted in greater overall team performance outcomes. Quite frankly, giving them the edge.

Why do we struggle with consistency in our day-to-day management?

The intuition of Dr Stuart Wilkinson to place more emphasis on the less flamboyant aspects of the game was developed to counter the tendency for human beings to chase the flashy plays and actions – the quick, adrenaline-fuelled outcomes we all wish to produce – while often neglecting the fundamentals.

We want the adrenaline and the best aspects that the tip (10 per cent) of performance or achievement can provide without the mundane, often unacknowledged elements of behaviour and commitment (90 per cent). For example, we bask in positive acknowledgement and praise, but we struggle when we do not see quick results for our investment or get the external validation we crave and desire. (See Figure 7.3.)

Why is this? Well, people rarely acknowledge our efforts below the surface as they are not always objectively linked to success, so we do not hold ourselves to account for them. However, what people fail to appreciate is that the largely hidden structure (the mundane) that lies below needs constant maintenance to assure buoyancy, allowing the glorious iceberg tip to stand proud and bask in the sunshine.

Figure 7.3 What they don't see nor give you credit for

Lesson 4

The psychological hardwiring we must 'hack' into and a counter-notion of failure

---

Before we continue, I hope you have realised ...

Motivation and desire come and go, regardless of how much you think you may want something. At some point, more often than not, motivation leaves the building – often through mental fatigue – allowing disillusionment to creep in. Routine discipline, underpinned by guilt, must become deeply embedded in order to become habitual: innate behaviour that upholds alignment to goals and successful outcomes.

Self-discipline and mental adaptability are the keys to success. It is doing the same old stuff, day in, day out, whether you are enjoying it or not. That is the key, just turning up, even if you are only going through the motions, and trusting the process. If you are relying on motivation, it is too elusive ... and you have already failed!

Maintaining alignment and assuring performance is not about riding the wave of motivation – that is always going to crash whether you like it or not. No, it is about constructing routines that become so entrenched they will withstand the torrent of disillusionment and fatigue when adversity strikes and motivation dissipates (see Figure 7.4). It is about creating the 'back stop'.

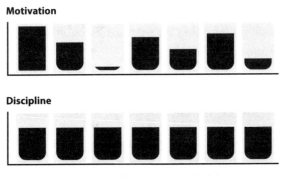

Rely on discipline, not on motivation

Figure 7.4 Don't count on motivation. Count on discipline

Why is something that seems so simple so hard to instil and maintain?

Over generations, human beings have developed ways to find 'cognitive' short cuts. From an evolutionary perspective, back when we were hunter-gatherers this strategy conserved our attentional resources (energy), ensuring our survival when food was scarce. Many of these prehistoric cognitive structures are still within us today and to a large extent they help us to navigate the social world efficiently.

However, they are outdated and invite laziness and complacency, which does not assure successful outcomes during complex goal acquisitions nor facilitate the application of attention to detail or its regular implementation to make a significant difference. This requires time and investment. But you need to know this about the seemingly insignificant things that people don't think will make a difference: they are the building blocks of unbelievable success and fulfilment.[6]

Attention to detail must be all-inclusive and applied consistently to all aspects of life, becoming a calling and a way of living. Any small lapses put holes in its integrity and without habitual patching, the whole structure risks losing its resilience, leading to 'behavioural derailment'. Fundamentally, attention to detail epitomises the notion of delayed gratification: putting in continuous effort for a payoff that is often months if not years down the line.

The second you start accepting instant gratification and you let it snowball, the attention to detail framework slips. It cannot be upheld without self-discipline. It is similar to training exceptionally hard in the gym, only to go home every night and not eat correctly – convincing yourself that because you have been to the gym, you deserve calorie-dense food, dessert or alcohol. If you desire significant results, you must delay gratification in this case to the weekend, or even every two weeks.

While training to fight UFC champion Khabib Nurmagomedov, Conor McGregor highlighted the importance of discipline and attention to detail if you want to achieve success. For example, don't say you are going to bed at 10 p.m. and then not do it, or if you are not supposed to have a dessert, don't go ahead and eat one anyway. 'That is the start of mental weakness,' said McGregor. 'What you say, you must do.' If you do not commit fully after a training session, he warned, 'it just impacts everything and snowballs down. I'm one hundred per cent committed in the gym, but it's the little touches out of it [that are important]'.[7]

Sacrifice is hard, delayed gratification is hard, trusting the process is hard and so is everything that comes with it: the disillusionment, the setbacks, the performance regression and the battle with self-confidence. However, I have found that no matter how tough things were, or how fraught my preconceptions were of a difficult journey towards achievement, it was never as bad as I expected. There was always something daily that I found enjoyable, which lifted me up and reinforced my rationale and purpose.

Maintaining ongoing action: inverted visualisation and parallel thinking

Much has been written about the need to add value to our goals in an attempt to hang on to motivation and ensure success. Many champion this method as a solid way of fortifying the stimulus, the end goal. For example, reinforcing through forward visualisation why you want to achieve the goal, how it will improve your life and the opportunities it will deliver. However, recent studies[8] focusing on cognitive strategies to predict success through ongoing action have found that one should reverse visualise instead. Write down what failure looks like before and during the acquisition process: how it makes you feel, the impact it would have on your self-concept and whether you are willing to accept it. In this notion, instead of looking forward, you keep looking back to what you are leaving behind and why – hence, 'inverted visualisation'.

According to Alexei Janssen, a top learning and performance coach who spent seventeen years coaching Royal Marines and Special Forces operators, all elite performers hold two conflicting beliefs at once, which makes them surprisingly irrational.

1. Total belief in the self: I will pass and get to the end. The likelihood is 100 per cent.

2. Acknowledgement that failure is a likely outcome: I might not pass. The likelihood seems more like 50–50.

For example, 'I am 100 per cent sure I will pass and get to the end. I just know it. There is absolutely no way I am leaving here without a Green Beret. But I might not. It is hard. If I don't pass, then so be it – I will go and do something else. But that is not going to happen because I already know it is in the bag. I can do this.'[9]

For Alexei, the Royal Marines recruits who harnessed this irrational thinking approach were almost 'bombproof'. 'They pushed on with total self-belief, but if they failed at something, got pushed back or injured, they did not fall apart.' Likewise, those recruits who struggled psychologically appeared to hold only one of the two belief structures.

Those who believed in only the first statement tended to suffer from self-induced pressure on tests and were more likely to over-react if they encountered failure, bad luck or something not going their way. Those who believed in only the second statement often lacked the conviction to get them through the very hard times.

Janssen's observations appear to show a tangible correlation between cognitive flexibility and success. How elite performers can visualise success, underpinned by an intrinsic self-confidence, while acknowledging that misfortune and adversity are uncontrollable but not final. That they will find a way to overcome such encounters and regather momentum.[10]

This remarkable observation depicts an ultimate belief in the self and one's ability to harness resolve, while acknowledging that external factors are, in essence, uncontrollable. In that sense, elite performers appear to detach the self from the unknown external factors incumbent in all aspects of life. In doing so, they possess enough flexibility in thought to overcome adversity and by default find comfort in uncertainty.

I find this fascinating. While engaged in Royal Marines training, I always turned to my interpretation of failure during my lowest points. When motivation was not there and I felt particularly low – to the point where I wanted to go home – I visualised failure and all the negatives that came with it. Despite how much I was hurting and the depth of disillusionment I was experiencing, failure kept me in the game and on course, until motivation and a more rational perspective returned.

Reflecting on all the ways in which we could fall short on the journey towards our goals is fundamental and allows us to prepare mentally for what is to come. The swift and potentially mentally damaging outcome of (definitive) failure is often the sole outcome, a personal choice that is frequently underpinned by a lack of preparation.

Remember, there is a reason why you want to take a particular course of action. It is often because you do not like the options on the table or you want to improve. Whatever the reason, the journey towards that aim is often littered with uncertainty and obstacles, but as I discussed in Phase Two, the anti-climax of success, growth and experience happens on the journey. It is not waiting at the finish line.

I lost motivation so many times during Royal Marines training, even at week twenty-six with only six weeks to go. Despite wanting that goal so badly, at times I just did not want to be there. I was so mentally and physically fatigued – almost broken – and this had the potential to sabotage my ambitions. However, during such periods I resorted constantly to the realisation of failure. I desperately did not want to validate the negative opinions of others who thought that I could not do it, nor did I want to re-inherit that previous life. I was determined not to let those people win and have the last laugh at my expense. I was in control of my own destiny and I made it so.

When motivation departed, the weight of failure scared me to death. It was so powerful that despite how disillusioned I became, I could not quit. The thought of failure kept me so anchored in that pursuit, it was the mental construct of stability that I never knew I had. During raw adversity, mental fatigue and disillusionment, failure became a reliable best friend, the friend I never knew I needed, that would never allow me to give up. In that sense, barring injury, the outcome of completing training was an absolute formality.

How does failure make you feel? Write down up to five outcomes that would likely materialise if you failed to attain your chosen goal or pursuit. What life choices or options would you likely re-inherit and why are you running away from them?

Remember, failure is often the outcome of personal choice. Whether you choose to entertain it is down to you and you alone. The alternative approach is perseverance. The two options produce totally different outcomes. (See Figure 7.5.)

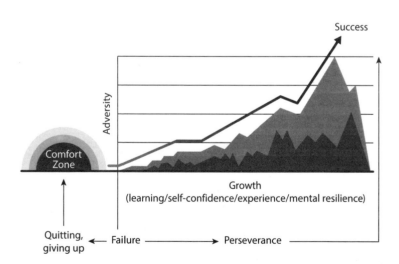

Figure 7.5 The power of perseverance

PRACTICAL APPLICATIONS

- Learning to arrive at acceptance quickly is fundamental to maintaining effective performance outcomes, a key construct of mental resilience, cognitive flexibility and adaptability.

- The 1 per cent outcomes are elicited via the implementation of a systematic attention to detail framework and upheld by consistency, a lifestyle underpinned by strategic routines, self-discipline and adherence to the notion of delayed gratification.

- Delayed gratification is a mental skill, an unequal relationship where the practitioner must invest time and energy into the journey, without any proper guarantee of return from the end goal.

- All high performers that achieve sustained success do so through consistent investment, under the pretext that the reward will be acquired at some point in the future. That is tough going. It is called 'trusting the process'.

- Maintaining performance and behavioural output when you are motivated is easy. The problem is what happens to consistency when you are not – often the result of fatigue. That is why it is so important to establish solid routines, underpinned by self-discipline that facilitates an 'internal trigger' for ongoing action. Therefore, the anchor that holds you steady and stops consistency slipping should *not* be constructed out of what is to gain but what is to lose and thus re inherit if we fail.

- The art of consistency is about showing up when it is hard, gruelling and painstaking, and when you simply do not feel like it but you commit anyway. For example, when you are sleep deprived.

- If harnessed correctly, failure can become the best friend you never thought you had or needed. Rather than focusing on the benefits of success, consider what behaviours lead to abject failure and how that makes you feel. Then avoid it.

CHAPTER EIGHT

Phase Five:
The Resilience Paradox

In 2011, I finally embarked on a career in private security. The exploration of this career path had led to an interview for a close protection role with Roman Abramovich's former wife and children. The salary was £55,000 a year and I desperately wanted the job.

However, once I spoke to my good friend John Riddle, who was still serving in the Royal Marines, he said, 'Mate, chin the Abramovich job off – the bloke's a c**t. Get in touch with Orlando Rogers at Solace. He's setting up a private maritime security company called Solace Global Maritime Limited due to the massive upsurge in piracy in and around Somalia. He's looking for lads who are ex-FSRT and will get you straight down for an interview.'

I called Orlando and after a brief chat he invited me for an interview the next day. I scrambled a suit together and went down to Poole. I had the interview on Tuesday, he offered me a job on Wednesday and on the Friday I flew out to Salalah in Oman.

It was surreal, that Monday I had been in Asda tallying up what was on the conveyor belt and fighting off anxiety as the total bill was approaching £30, knowing that anything over and I would have to endure the embarrassment of putting back food, which had become a regular occurrence since leaving the Marines. Then, after flying out on Friday and arriving in Durban, South Africa, ten days later I had earned £4,500 including travel and expenses.

As maritime security operators, we were armed and worked in two- to four-man teams. We embarked on vessels from the Suez Canal, south down the Red Sea, across the Gulf of Aden into the Somali Basin, then north through the Indian Ocean in line with Muscat, and finally east as far as Sri Lanka and south to Durban, South Africa. This area was known as the HRA (high-risk area).

The work was mind-numbingly boring in a lot of ways. We were either up on the bridge on watch or down below sleeping, watching movies, or hammering the gym or anything else that could be used to provide elements of resistance equipment, which was very much dependent on the ship. But the money to be earned was outrageous and this was fundamental to the job.

Once I had been paid for my first transit and that money landed in my account, I more or less stayed out for nine months solid with a two-week break (taken only because my brain was fried with fatigue), earning ridiculous amounts of money cross-decking from vessel to vessel as they went through the HRA. However, it was during this period that I started experiencing cognitive fatigue and for the first time in my life I lacked the ability to apply the resilience to withstand and come through attritional fatigue in order to control my emotions, something I had always been good at before.

Environmental fatigue was also wreaking havoc on my senses. The stark contrast between living conditions on board ship and the predominantly Middle Eastern countries that we inhabited had a massive impact on my ability to stay fresh and preserve and rejuvenate my cognitive resources.

What became apparent during the months that followed was that I began to worry irrationally about my health, a form of hypochondria. While on board ship, I became obsessed with the almost frantic urge to check what I thought were lumps, bumps and various other physical and non-physical signs of disease. Sounds bizarre, I know, but at times this consumed me as I tried to hide my checking and accompanying trance-like state from my teammates.

There was a significant turning point when my OCD (Obsessive Compulsive Disorder) switched from being an ally (perfectionist) to my enemy (antagonist). I sent an email to the company operations manager to update him on our situation while in transit. The following day I received a reply and reviewing my own email I saw that I had made multiple spelling mistakes, the grammar and punctuation were shocking, and quite frankly I couldn't believe I had sent it. I had just been made Team Leader, Hence the reason I was sending situation reports to HQ, so this was damningly significant. I desperately wanted to appear competent and switched on in all aspects. This email made me look anything but that. As the months passed, that one mistake ended up creating a monster of mental torment, which resulted in cognitive debilitation as I tried to harness the strength to push on. I thought that if I blindly 'soldiered on', I would eventually ride it out. How wrong I was.

It was not only the resilience required to stay out, it was having to be constantly alert to the environment and the threats it posed – for example, the threat of pirate attack, or the threat of a road traffic accident (RTA) in the region, which was one of the biggest threats if we embarked or disembarked in Egypt.

Operating in some of the countries I did during this period and the years that followed was in stark contrast to the comfort and risk-free surroundings of the UK, which we often take for granted. These countries, as well as the living conditions on some of the vessels, attacked the senses and required the utmost application of mental resilience, which was often a daily struggle.

The *Vogebulker*

Given the number of times I transited through the HRA in 2011, I had an acute awareness that at some stage I was going to be attacked by pirates. Then at 6.30 p.m. on 6 August, while under way heading south down the Red Sea, a 300-metre bulk carrier named the *Vogebulker* came under attack. The time had come.

A few days earlier, before boarding the vessel, I had flown out to Malta to collect weapons and ops kit from an armoury. Maritime security companies utilised various armouries around the HRA to store weapons and ops kit to save staff from trying to get them through international customs. Approaching the *Vogebulker* in the pilot boat, it was clear that it was a massive target, which immediately made me feel uneasy. It was heavily laden with iron ore with a 5-metre freeboard, meaning it was so low in the water you could come alongside and step on board. When the captain informed me that the maximum speed was only 7 knots at best (about 10 mph), I knew that this was creating the perfect recipe for the vessel to be a prime target for pirates.

We picked up the rest of my team in Port Suez, Egypt, four days later and then we were off. Luckily, the security measures on the vessel were amazing, with numerous physical barriers to deter the efforts of a pirate or non-compliant boarding attempt. Measures included razor wires around the outer edge of the deck to prevent access by ladders, as well as on both external starboard and portside stairways, which led directly to the bridge. Also the creation of a citadel, an internal safe house usually constructed in the engine room, with medical supplies, satellite or hardwired telecommunications, dry food, water and so on

Despite all this, I still had an uncomfortable feeling. My gut was telling me that this was our time as we sailed down the Red Sea towards the Bab-el-Mandeb. One of my lads was an ex-SBS coxswain and he was joking that he *wanted* to get attacked. He wanted to see some action.

Against company policy, I told the lads to keep their AK-47s loaded, out of the secure boxes and on the side of the bridge wings. This was a strict no-no and I could have lost my job over it, but it felt like the right thing to do. The night of the attack, I was having dinner with the captain and chief officer when one of the lads radioed me. His words will stay with me forever. 'Gaz, there are two skiffs coming at us at speed. Get up here now!'

I jumped up, my food and cutlery flying up in the air, and rushed up about a dozen flights of stairs faster than I'd have thought possible. When I got to the bridge, one of the lads helped me into my body armour, while another passed me the binoculars. I could feel the adrenaline surging through my system, threatening to preclude me from any form of normal, composed breathing or rational thinking. I was the team leader and I had to stay calm and collected, but I am not ashamed to say that I was terrified.

After a couple of deep breaths and an internal conversation with myself, I looked through the binoculars. I knew straight away we were about to be boarded and I am not sure what shocked me the most: the crews of the skiffs jumping around with AKs and RPGs in their hands, or the young lad lying on the front of one of the skiffs as if he was sunbathing.

In situations like this, you don't know if it is real. You can see the boats approaching, their speed and angle of approach look threatening, and for all intents and purposes it is absolutely hostile behaviour. But you get caught in a middle ground of asking yourself, 'Is this actually happening? Are we about to get contacted? Are they fishermen or are they coming to sell us something?' This was not uncommon while sailing through narrow passages of water at sea.

Obviously, a misjudgement on the 'Shit, we're going to be attacked' scale comes with massive consequences if you feel compelled to react with force. The main issue here is that once in, you are in – much like a street fight, where once engaged you have to see it through – and you have to win or the outcome will be terrible. When using weapons, the stakes are also significantly higher, with death being the likely alternative if you fail. All these scenarios pass through your brain in split seconds as your eyes desperately try to establish an accurate bearing on reality.

My autopilot kicked in and I told the captain to send the crew to the citadel, the vessel's safe room, taking all the mobile phones and laptops they could get their hands on. I told the chief officer to make a radio 'Mayday' transmission to United Kingdom Maritime Trade Operations (UKMTO) to try to get one of the few Coalition Naval warships to scramble to our aid.

My team took up their defensive positions behind cover along the starboard side of the bridge wing. Once the skiffs were within range of us (300 metres), I gave the order to fire warning shots into the water in front of their approach. The sound from the

AKs discharging was deafening as it echoed off the steel structure of the vessel. The shots were made tactically to show that we had serious weapons on board and were using live ammunition as, unbelievably, some ships did not have either in these waters. My Royal Marines experience had taught me what it must feel like to try boarding a vessel while under fire, so I was convinced that this would make them back off.

Instead, I could not believe it when they made further advances and began circling around us. Then, to our horror, more were arriving in the distance from both the port and starboard sides. This was probably the only time in my life when I thought we were going to get killed.

Being in a position where I thought I was going to die is something I never want to experience again. It was a truly awful few seconds where I simply didn't know what to do. In this mental state I was reduced to being a child wanting to call my mum – an embarrassing revelation that I never disclosed during or after the engagement. In that split-second of panic, I lost control of my most reliable weapon: my mind. I came face to face with a panic-stricken, inner fragility that I had never encountered before. I desperately did not want to die and for a few seconds I felt we should surrender to save what percentage of life we had left in our favour. No sooner had I contemplated that thought, however, than I quickly came to my senses and tuned back into the live environment. This took charge and I became fully aware of what we needed to do, which was fight them hard and with maximum aggression.

The skiffs were approaching fast and the previous ones were still circling, so we fought on. I told one team member, Ben, to man the starboard side and lay down warning fire. I then ran to the port side and instructed another team member, John, to do the same. However, the pirates were now approaching us from the rear as well, a tactic used by the Royal Marines boarding teams. For example, one or two boats will circle the vessel and make dummy side approaches, while others target the rear, moving faster in oxygenated water generated from the ship's propellers, and attempt to board using ladders. Their understanding of this tactical manoeuvre was very good, but so was mine from my time with the FSRT.

After a few deep breaths, I had the clearest and most vital connection to my environment that I have ever had in my life. I literally could have heard a pin drop. It was as if my brain was operating at its fullest potential and I felt more alive than I knew was possible.

I sent the last member of my team up to the top of the monkey deck, the highest point on the ship to gain a 360 degree perspective, and he relayed the pirates' positions and movements back to me via radio so that the rest of us on the lower deck could respond accordingly. For thirty-five minutes, the four of us repelled twelve skiffs full of pirates trying to board and take control of our vessel. It was absolutely incredible. Poor Ben, who had just left close protection operations in Iraq for an easy and safer life, got caught up in one of the biggest and most aggressive pirate attacks of that year. Luckily, we were able to laugh about it for days afterwards.

The captain and crew were elated and threw us a massive party the night before we disembarked. I went to bed early, but I heard that it got wild. A few days later, we found out that a Somali newspaper had reported the attack and had placed bounties on our heads.

I have thought about this attack and my initial reaction to it ever since. After all the training and urging for contact, had

I really crumbled under the pressure during this most testing period in my life? After all, we got the result and we repelled the attack. Maybe my 'cognitive dissonance' created by the perceived realisation of imminent death elicited feelings that were entirely natural, human emotions that we all experience in such overwhelming situations.

The reality is that I have never spoken about this to anyone until now, but it demonstrates the importance of cultivating mental toughness. Ultimately, this was the classic example of the fight or flight response. Flight here was not an option. It rarely is in such situations, yet your mind does venture there in an effort to try to preserve life. Once I had acknowledged that no one else was responsible for getting us out of this situation, I accepted that fighting was our only way out, which flipped the mental switch from flight to fight.

Midway through the contact, I realised that we were gradually winning the battle and defending ourselves to success. At this point I felt pure and undiluted euphoria. From thinking that we were going to die to knowing we were going to survive was the most powerful and intoxicating moment I have ever had in my life.

Lesson 5

Behaviour inducing stress awareness: does resilience really protect us?

What we call mental resilience is merely an individual's degree of emotional control at any given moment and the cognitive endurance to maintain required behaviours in line with adverse external demands.

For example, in the exposure to SERE (Survival, Evasion, Resistance and Escape) training for elite military personnel, during Special Forces selection, soldiers are subjected to 'resistance to interrogation' methods. These include sensory deprivation, cold water exposure, stress positions, and listening to excruciating noises and music via headphones, such as babies crying, fingernails scraping down a chalkboard, or the likes of Barney Rubble singing happy birthday ... on repeat. All of which induce the desirable effect: sleep deprivation and extreme fatigue.

Once those on selection arrive here, the aim is no longer to weed out the unsuitable – they have already left. The purpose of this phase is to expose future Special Forces operators to the very darkest realities of warfare, in order to prepare for such eventualities and ultimately preserve life.

'Process' here is the key word. Both the US and UK military are aware that you cannot simply throw someone into this stressful environment because you perceive them to be an 'emotionless' soldier. You need to introduce them gradually to the exposure via a controlled process, which is as follows: Classroom phase (mental preparation) > Evade (controlled mental conditioning) > Detection (exposure to the 'desired' lived experience).[1]

This process is called stress inoculation or vaccination: to 'vaccinate' people to extreme stress so they can handle it better in future. However, 'the first step isn't to throw someone into the deep end of extreme stress; it is teaching the skills necessary'[2] to cope at each incremental phase before turning up the intensity and moving on to the next phase. But crucially, this tailored approach and the subsequent teachings work only for that specific lived experience. You cannot copy and paste this experience to another highly stressful or grief-stricken life encounter, such as the sudden and uncontrollable breakdown of a long-term relationship or the loss of a family member, and expect it to be effective.

Likewise, you could not jump straight to phase three and expect success because you have had success in other stress-related encounters, much like you would not jump in the deep end of a swimming pool without learning then practising the fundamentals of swimming.[3]

Yet we believe the application of resilience – underpinned by social expectation – can be applied like an emotional shield to all of life's curve balls, and this simply is not the case. If it were, the military would not invest in the process of stress inoculation for SERE training, as well as other potentially stressful and life-threatening encounters like Dunker Drills – helicopter underwater escape training.

While we often attach resilience to someone's ability to endure such conditions or difficult life periods, with a degree of longevity being the key component, calling this resilience and believing it protects is dangerous. Because we demand strength from resilience, it is an expectation – the flip side of which is weakness, where something let's say man-made loses its structural integrity, and we cannot accept that. Let's face it, we never want anything to break. Right?

When we frantically attach our expectation of resilience to human behaviour, we create an issue. The successful application of resilience in the face of adversity is incredibly valued because strength is valued. It is something that elicits awe and fascination in all of us. We admire it and want to attain it, and in the process it becomes a highly sought-after social currency.

Weakness is never good enough in anything. It denotes a risk, but more so, a liability that we try desperately to avoid. Therefore we uphold the qualities of resilience by acting in a resilient way,[4] which further compromises our cognitive mechanisms. To our detriment, we have conceptualised emotional

119

regulation and cognitive endurance as resilience, probably to simplify the complexity. Where we accept the limitations of physical endurance to varying degrees in different people, while acknowledging the need to 'taper' (*wind down and rest*) to stay at the top physically, we cannot accept the limitations of mental resilience because it is perceived to be rigid and should not lose its strength or break.

Resilience is an absolute expectation and sadly, that is where we often fall short and venture deeper into catastrophic burnout, much like a car losing traction and sliding uncontrollably off the road. In slow motion, you know where you are heading, but taking corrective action is now ineffective. You are going!

We have been mis-sold. We have been aspiring to attain such qualities, thinking that once resilient, we will continue to be so; that it makes us resilient to *all* of life's challenges. In an abstract way, we believe resilience is a one-size-fits-all construct. Therefore we generalise such assumptions in a faulty belief system that people who appear to possess mental toughness are indeed resilient and thus in some way unaffected by the rest of life's challenges.

Although humans are adaptable in thought, and with adequate training and certain exposures we can acquire more resilience, it has a breaking strain without due care and attention. There is a point at which it loses its integrity and, in doing so, opens the floodgates to mental health issues. For example, imagine a man-made watertight door: the seal is what keeps it integral and upholds its integrity. However, if not maintained, greased and inspected regularly, it will start to let in water and the whole structure will eventually become compromised.

A forensic deconstruction of resilience and the need to acknowledge it as 'cognitive endurance'

In its current form, we believe that resilient people remain resilient. Well, thinking about it logically, resilience is cognitive endurance repackaged, which itself is an adaptation to external demand: a stimulus. People become conditioned to adversity, whether objective (environmental) or subjective (internal perception).

Mental conditioning that results in toughness or resilience (*cognitive endurance*) is no different from the laws of physical conditioning. The more you subject your body to load, impact and resistance, the less of an effect 'delayed onset muscle soreness' (DOMS) has on the body. The same applies to the mind. When the stimulus is removed and mental adaptation is no longer needed to that extreme, then conditioning and thus resilience will decline.

My point is that whenever physical or mental adversity is stimulating the mind, the mind will naturally adapt, and for a period the outcome will be that one becomes more mentally robust. Likewise, if someone withdraws from adversity and resides in momentary or prolonged comfort, the mind will go back closer to the baseline. A place where even life's basic existence can appear challenging. Therefore, mental resilience and toughness require constant investment (*conditioning*) and maintenance, and a failure to do so will result in mental weakness, reacting negatively to day-to-day commitments.

In this notion, mental toughness or resilience is only borrowed, therefore it is in a constant state of flux and susceptible to infiltration if we are not introspective and do not learn to self-regulate effectively.

On the one hand, the notion of resilience is valued and conceptualised as one's ability to endure suffering and to display mental toughness via the enactment of the behavioural manifestations that follow. This is a potentially dangerous internal and external expectation, which attempts to strip away our emotions, in the sense that applying resilience or cognitive endurance should not hurt. It does hurt, in the same way that physical endurance hurts, and to deny that it does not is to neglect what we experience being human.

On the other hand, resilience cannot remain resilient and at some point it loses its integrity, whether resilience is defined as an objective or subjective representation, such as a piece of steel or the mind. Our current expectations leave no room for periodic fragility or vulnerability. Let's face it, find anyone's Achilles heel and it will derail them from their persona of resilience. I am not saying that resilience is not useful; of course it is. It helps during certain situations and exposure to adverse experiences can build resilience. However, when we apply resilience, consciously or subconsciously, we are, by default, experiencing emotional discomfort. Hence its application, and rationally that must have an adverse effect, which starts to hammer away at our emotional defences.

Speaking personally, people often think that I must have done some taboo things in my military and private security career that required impregnable mental resilience and strength. Likewise, they would say I have been through some extraordinary experiences that must have resulted in more resilience or de-sensitisation to daily stresses as a by-product. Their appraisals are wrong. Yes, I may have done some taboo things and had some truly unbelievable experiences, but half the time, I was only *acting* in a resilient way. I was keeping my fear sub-surface because that was what was expected of me under the guise of what we call 'role schemes' – shared information about social roles and occupational expectations.[5]

View the application of resilience like the use of ammunition

The weapon (*mind*) is nothing without ammunition (*attentional resources*). Without each other, both entities are ineffective. When brought together, however, the impact is devastating – like the relationship between a firearm and a bullet.

It is easy to discharge all one's ammunition in a semi- or fully automatic firearm and it is often irresistible. But trigger control and experience are necessary to conserve ammunition (*cognitive/attentional resources*). It requires an acknowledgement of the bigger picture and the ability to resist the temptation to empty the tank. If you discharge it all, you have nothing left. Its use should be strategic and applied in controlled bursts with poise and precision. A lack of control and respect, and you will end up with a lump of metal in your hands that is ineffective and pointless. Therefore, it is essential to factor in planned rest.

Acknowledging the contradiction of resilience is essential to finding the sweet spot:

1. To become more resilient, you must continuously punch through the pain barrier.

2. To avoid resilience burnout, you must prioritise rest, sleep and relaxation.

Resilience, as we know and apply it, is an imposter. Influenced by social expectation, it eventually leads us into mental illness. So it is imperative that we rebrand resilience as 'cognitive endurance', allowing us to acknowledge our mental limitations. This will enable the development of greater and more sustainable applications of cognitive endurance in order to counter stress emergence and burnout rather than the continuous misuse of resilience that we currently employ.

PRACTICAL APPLICATIONS

- Delayed gratification through the application of cognitive endurance is all well and good, but when that is applied to all our personal comforts, it can be detrimental.

- We must acknowledge the limitations of our own psychology and look to rebrand resilience as cognitive endurance. In doing so, it will not only help us to detect and avoid the emergence of stress and mental illness, it will also preserve performance for longer.

- Stress inoculation is vital to prepare people for stressful situations. However, each exposure is specific and inoculation does not vaccinate against all stress or traumatic encounters, just as resilience does not shield us from all facets of life's adversity, especially for prolonged periods, without an impact on our emotional wellbeing.

- People who constantly apply continuous resilience often fail to take notice of the detrimental warning signs.

Pushing and pushing at the cost of our mental wellbeing and health balance will eventually lead to stress, cognitive exhaustion and the emergence of mental illness.

- Factoring in planned rest and recuperation is essential, but this must be scheduled into a strategic performance or lifestyle framework sooner – ideally during 'Phase Four: Maintaining Behavioural Alignment' – to mitigate the potentially aggressive descent into cognitive exhaustion and even deeper into burnout.

CHAPTER NINE

Phase Six: Cognitive Exhaustion

My eyes have just opened and once again, to my horror, I have arrived back in this world to be assaulted by an uncontrollable, intrusive thought, relating to my death. Each night, as my anxiety gradually subsides, I hope and pray it has left me for good, that it was only temporary and I am somehow getting better, returning to the person I was before.

People seem to think I am fearless, that I appear to thrive in war-torn environments and I could likely kill anyone, unfazed, with my bare hands. The reality is that I have completely lost control of my ability to regulate my thoughts and emotions. I feel scared and vulnerable in society; my mind is in free-fall and no matter how frantically I pull the ripcord, my parachute will not open.

Due to the prolonged lack of action and often mind-numbing boredom during my months at sea as a maritime security officer, my mental health struggles persisted, slowly getting worse as time went on. After working for extremely long periods in semi-hostile waters, I took a new role spearheading close-protection operations in Egypt, during the Arab Spring and Egyptian Revolution. Although this work was not at all taxing or hostile in any sense (in fact, it was a dream of a job), that was where my OCD became really destructive and debilitating.

In short, another colleague and I were deployed in Cairo for six weeks at a time. We were there to protect and escort Shell International Trading and Shipping Company senior executives who were travelling to and from Port Suez to conduct vessel inspections, prior to them sailing south down the Red Sea towards the IRTC (Internationally Recommended Transit Corridor) off the coast of Somalia. In a week, we probably did two tasks at the most, but it was not the workload that affected me, it was the abundance of 'alone time' spent in our hotel rooms.

I started checking things. Silly and irrational things like light switches, even though I could see if they were on or off, because I stopped trusting the information that was coming in from my own eyes. For example, the room is dark, so the light is off. It caused my mind to snowball, sabotaging my ability to regulate my thoughts and emotions, which in turn opened the door to some disturbing and intrusive thoughts.

From a rational perspective, I knew this was all bullshit. I could see that the tap was off and the water was off, or the light switch was in the off position, but I could not stop checking them. In an attempt to regain control, I would count to ten. That was meant to be the cut-off point to stop the checking, exit the trance-like state and go about my business. But the urges were so strong that ten became twenty and so on, often keeping me frozen in place for minutes and sometimes up to an hour.

I cannot express how awful this place was. I felt severely mentally ill and I thought I would never get better. I would lie on my bed, or go and meet my colleagues during meal times, and dreadful thoughts would keep dropping into my head without warning. These thoughts all related to dying, often in the most disturbing and bizarre ways conceivable. For example, while laying on my bed I would look out of the window, which was several floors up, to a hotel building opposite, and picture myself falling off the top floor of the building.

It didn't end there. I could imagine it so vividly, I would get butterflies envisioning the fall, then physically close my eyes and tense up as the ground approached, ending with a sudden, full-body jolt as I hit the ground. It was absolutely horrifying and this was happening constantly, to the point where I would close my eyes and not want to look at anything at all, in case my mind constructed another event.

It also happened during lunch and dinner. I would eat something and envision choking, which then triggered panic attacks. All while I was sitting with my colleagues, trying to avoid eye contact in an attempt to maintain the facade of nothing being wrong.

During this period, I was so cognitively impaired due to stress and anxiety, I could not articulate properly. It was so distressing that I had to think of what I was going to say and rehearse the sentence structure beforehand. When it came to the actual encounter, it felt as if my mouth was not moving properly. I would get the words wrong, stutter, or make an absolute mess of what I was trying to say, which made me look stupid in front of people. Sometimes I could not recall words effortlessly and would have to substitute one word for another that didn't fit or make the sentence flow. It would make zero sense, which created even more anxiety and stress. It was truly awful and such a vicious circle. I had to try to bring conscious awareness to my thinking in order to differentiate between the fake, irrational thoughts and the rational ones.

I needed to regain control, so I tried the following four steps:

- To identify the cognitive distortions and automatic negative thoughts and what triggered them.

- To dispute and engage with these thoughts consciously in a critical manner.

- To counter and replace such thoughts with a more positive or rational appraisal of a particular event.

- To immediately challenge irrational thoughts with the key phrase: 'It's false emotion.' I did this one a lot and it helped.

In March 2013, I was undertaking my final rotation in Egypt, while experiencing these growing mental health struggles. This all coincided with a long-awaited job offer and impending deployment to Afghanistan as a close-protection operator for the US Department of Defense. I had applied for three years to get onto the Hostile Environment Close Protection (HECP) circuit in Iraq or Somalia, called 'The Sandpit'.

During the early days of applications, all of which were unsuccessful, I had never considered Afghanistan. That territory was completely off limits for me; there was no chance I was going there. But then something changed. This sudden switch in desire ignited an extremely challenging mental space, one that I never want to experience again.

While training in the Royal Marines, it was the thought of deploying to Afghanistan that kept me engaged and wanting to become a Royal Marines Commando. I desperately wanted to go there. Yet, during my time in the Royal Marines and despite the Corps commitments in Afghanistan, the opportunity never came. Having said that, during the initial twelve months after leaving Commando Training Centre, three of my original troop members, Tom Curry, Ben Whatley and Ben Reddy, were all killed in Afghanistan. This shattered my sense of invincibility very quickly. Quite frankly, I thought, if these guys can get killed, anyone can, and I became convinced that Afghanistan was a bad omen.

However, once I left the Marines, I could not live with myself for not going. I felt that I was a sell-out and it niggled away at me like a relentless inner voice. If not addressed, I knew I would regret not going for the rest of my life. Professionally, I was drawn to the place. It was, and still is, the ultimate testing ground for any military operator and I wanted to test and refine my skills in the toughest environment on the planet.

So I was absolutely scared to death about going to Afghanistan and this caused a Goliath of stress-induced, mental health issues, which further encouraged my intrusive thoughts. Yet at the same time I was furiously excited about it and wanting to tick off the experience – to live life in the rawest sense and operate with absolute purpose, with one goal in mind: survival, mankind's ultimate adventure.

This mental conflict, known in psychology as 'cognitive dissonance', resulted in me falling ever further into cognitive burnout in the weeks leading up to my deployment. While waiting to depart, I felt anything but the elite soldier and publicly held concept of a Royal Marines Commando. This unrelenting mental torment shattered my sense of who I was and who I needed to be to undertake that role, which made my whole identity a fraud. I remember sitting in my house in Wakefield and looking out of the window into the garden, thinking that the last place I should be going in ten days was Afghanistan.

How had it come to this? One thing I do know is that I had no alternative. I possessed a specific skillset that placed me in the very jobs and environments that were now making me ill. I must emphasise that this was not post-traumatic stress disorder (PTSD). I had reached a place of almost drastic and totally irrational hypersensitivity and hypervigilance, fuelled by an out-of-control OCD crisis that I did not know how to escape.

The result was that a lack of time off and constantly staying out there working – without acknowledging the warning signs – eventually compromised my mental health. But despite feeling mentally fatigued and ravaged with OCD, I continued to apply the resilience required to keep on doing the job. After all, that was what was expected of me, both by others and by myself. I needed to earn money and the longer I stayed out there, the more I learned and the reward was good. Also, taking time off meant that I would not be at the forefront of all the best jobs, so I would lose momentum. When I got the call, therefore, I almost had to say yes. In my mind, I needed to keep pushing, all the while abusing my cognitive resources and bleeding my resilience dry: my once superpower.

This was new territory for me. Not only had I abused my resilience to stay out and earn money, I didn't realise I would end up mentally ill, not for one minute. I thought the issues I was experiencing would subside long before that. However, during this period I knew it had all gone too far and that I was broken, to the point where I had to seek help. I recognised that I could not get out of this alone. Worryingly, I thought I would never get better.

This episode revealed the uncomfortable truth about my fragility for the first time in my life. Through reflection, I realised that spending sustained periods alone while completely cut off from the outside world was detrimental to my mental health.

Social isolation and extremely harsh environments invited all the negative aspects associated with my OCD.

Throughout my short career in the Royal Marines and in the years after when I engaged in private security overseas, I had ignored the mental warning signs of psychological fatigue and pushed on, often in direct conflict with my wellbeing. A defence mechanism, or so I thought, to withstand change and adversity and to mitigate the often uncontrollable, threat-induced situations. This enduring cycle prevented me from taking adequate rest, despite knowing that I needed it and yearning for some time out.

Instead, I pushed myself to stay consistent in all aspects of my life for fear of professional regression. This meant forcing myself to do job-related physical exercise even when I was severely run down and my immune system was shattered, resulting in outbreaks of cold sores and eczema under my eyes and between my fingers and toes. This has always marked the physical manifestation of fatigue for me, a point at which I have gone too far. I should have rested earlier, but until recently in my life, I never have.

In the past, I have been relentless in my pursuit, treating goal acquisition like an aggressive, uncompromising race to the finish line, meaning that I have neglected all my personal needs, then reloaded and gone straight to the start line of another challenge. In retrospect, I could have achieved the same but with a smarter approach. One with health and wellbeing front and centre, where I could have factored in some personal comforts without applying delayed gratification to everything, and still got the same results. For instance, I would not drink or go out, and on the odd occasion when I did, I felt really guilty. I studied, worked or trained throughout the weekends, so I never had any time off. It was not smart or sustainable.

Some of the drivers forcing a need for me to apply and uphold resilience have included an unrelenting thirst to succeed in all aspects of my life, driven by the fear of being average, but also my obsessive nature. Such drivers applied relentlessly have always resulted in cognitive burnout.

For me, and for many others with the growth mindset, the sacrifice of doing what you don't want to, such as attending the gym with consistency and enthusiasm or, like me, peeling myself away from the TV to study, is often a necessary evil. It is a non-negotiable duty that must be performed to mitigate the guilt of not doing it, the anxiety over losing career momentum or physical gains, and the depression at failing to stay consistent and regressing. It was also to control my mood regulation. In a sense, my day would feel tarnished if I did not undertake some form of personal development activity.

Delayed gratification – sacrificing comfort and convenience for better days ahead – is all well and good when applied in certain aspects to produce results. However, when applied to every single aspect of life, it quickly becomes detrimental and causes too much strain on resilience or mental endurance. In my lifestyle and occupational case, that meant literally stripping away every familiarity and comfort by being in sharply contrasting and hostile environments and thus being cut off from my family and friends and the comforts of the UK.

No matter how dedicated you are, everyone needs some element of comfort and familiarity in their life, whether it be social, personal relaxation, diet treats, hobbies, pastimes or so on. Prior to experiencing catastrophic burnout, I had nothing. Everything sparked an internal conflict and a compromise – and that eventually took its toll, as I will explain in the next chapter.

Lesson 6

Establishing an understanding of emotional monitoring

The relentless focus and dedication required to channel our attentional resources to achieve a goal, or to maintain sustained performance in challenging situations, at some point starts to create a mental strain, which impairs our nervous system. This not only affects our cognitive efficiency, and thus our performance, but it begins to sabotage our wellbeing.

When we start to become overwhelmed by demand and complexity, and forward focusing becomes problem centred as we try to predict the future, the mind becomes overloaded, leading to stress. Prolonged 'problem-centre' focus is a whole new beast. In an attempt to prepare the body for a perceived threat, the body releases excess cortisol into the bloodstream.[1] In doing so, it enhances the brain's usage of glucose (energy – often referred to as nervous energy) to prepare us for the classic fight-or-flight situation and to repair tissues.[2] Too much of this not only begins to cause health problems, it compromises your attentional resources. Imagine a university student. If their attention is undermined by stress, then their memory processing is affected = poor attention = poor short-term memory = less chance of processing short-term memory into longer-term memory. This results in a lack of ability to recall information on the course throughout subsequent stages. Hence the term 'brain fog'.

Long-term activation of this chronic stress response disrupts almost all of the body's nervous processing system, which catastrophically impairs the mind, fuels anxiety and results in underperformance.[3] Gazing into the future is important for planning and organising our lives. However, when that lens focuses on worries and assesses future outcomes negatively, things can quickly become a problem and compromise the mind.[4]

When it comes to our organ systems and bodily functioning, excess cortisol affects nearly all the organ systems: nervous, immune, cardiovascular, respiratory, reproductive, musculoskeletal and integumentary.[5] In terms of our performance capability and the fluidity of cognitive processes required to facilitate 'executive function' – our unique ability to monitor and adjust our behaviours to promote long-term goal acquisition – then being in a constant state of fight or flight 'changes immune system response and suppresses the digestive system, the reproductive system and growth processes'.[6]

Chronic stress can have the following negative effects. It:

- affects sleep

- creates fatigue

- suppresses appetite

- decreases productivity

- affects emotional regulation, leading to greater propensity for anger

- leads to anxiety and depression

- results in trouble concentrating

- leads to a loss of motivation and social withdrawal.

It goes without saying that all these and more inhibit our ability to maintain performance. But here is the problem. What if you are struggling mentally, like I was? You are aware that you need rest, time out and recuperation, but you cannot get off the horse due to work obligations or financial pressures.

Take a moment to think about your past or present worries, or let's call them fears. Very often they are not happening right here, right now. What is really happening is that you are thinking ahead about what 'might' be. You are conjuring up a multitude of scenarios that are creating emotional turmoil, when in fact, right now, none of that is happening.

I wrote this about the perception of fear in *Becoming the 0.1%*: 'Fear is a state of mind created by an illusionist, a trickster of emotion, which deceives our perception of an event – manipulating our emotions by constructing a version of reality that will likely never (statistically) happen.'

Controlling our emotions takes practice and skill, through experience and by resisting the temptation to succumb to emotion, but understand that fear, like worry, is an illusion created by the mind around an event that is yet to happen. It is testament to the fact that not all people feel fear and create anxiety about the same thing.

Therefore, the perception of fear is merely a prediction based on an individual interpretation of an event, which the mind tries desperately to evaluate. In doing so, it maximises the potential outcome to prepare the body for the unknown.

Introspection and de-regulating the nervous system

Ultimately, if you arrive at this point and then try to take mitigating action, it is probably too late, I'm afraid. Cognitive performance, goal pursuit or even just trying to manage your day-to-day routines effectively will have to take a back seat until you recover and rejuvenate your cognitive resources.

Understanding your own unique stress-triggers, and spotting the early warning signs of stress emergence, are absolutely essential. But this is often possible only through prior exposure to that 'specific' lived experience, which is stress. You need to have acquired such experience from being in that difficult place before.

In our daily lives, it is unlikely that such exposures will come via the 'benefit and process'-driven way of stress inoculation (as mentioned in the previous lesson). However, if we choose to be introspective and reflect on our past experiences, we can evaluate them and through a process of preparation and a sprinkling of resilience, learn how to cope better in future. We can also take mitigating steps to avoid chronic stress by developing and then maintaining a mental skills performance foundation.

In 2014, the RAND Corporation was tasked with preparing the US Air Force to perform better under stressful conditions. At the top of the list were the following cognitive performance skills they wished to safeguard during stressful situations:[7]

- ensuring self-confidence (in adversity)

- goal setting (ensuring executive function capability)

- attentional control (during stress)

- arousal control (harnessing composure during different environmental demands)

- imagery (the likes of vision and creativity)

- positive self-talk (to counter negative self-talk)

- compartmentalisation (breaking down adversity to make it more manageable and achievable from a mental perspective).

Even further, in an attempt to anticipate the exposure to unexpected stressors, militaries worldwide have begun to explore the field of positive psychology. Through the implementation of learning and strategies that are underpinned by wellbeing and mental health awareness, including 'learned optimism' and emotional regulation, the goal is to prepare soldiers to 'handle the specific stresses on the battlefield and stressors that hit us in everyday life'.[8]

Through a process of forward planning and emotional monitoring – systematically observing and recording thoughts, body feelings and emotions to control expressive behaviours – stress emergence can be identified and alleviated, affording a greater chance of maintaining cognitive effectiveness and thus performance for longer. Acknowledging the importance of psychological monitoring skills, the US Navy Seals implemented a classroom phase to their teachings of stress, trauma and performance during the early 2000s.[9]

That said, with certain professions or life events it is often unavoidable and sometimes inevitable that we arrive at cognitive exhaustion and performance becomes compromised. But there are things we can do to deregulate the nervous system.

It is quite easy to follow the generic advice at this point and tell you to practise mindfulness-type techniques in order to deregulate the nervous system. But let's face it, while they are said to work, I find the practice and application of such methods to be tedious, and I am not alone. This worries me, because mindfulness requires a lot of interpretation from a subconscious perspective and, crucially, its benefits are rarely, if ever, observable. As human beings, we struggle with subjectivity, which makes it very hard to establish consistent routines and effective habits.

What the military does well

Royal Marines perform at such a high standard because rest and operational commitments are cycled: for instance, four to six months on operations, six to eight weeks off, six weeks specialised training, six to eight weeks pre-deployment training, two weeks off, and so on. Yet in the civilian world, it seems to be the complete opposite. No strategic cycling, merely relentless work and often no strategic holidays or time off until it is too late.

According to the new tech start-up Loopin, a peak performance and workplace wellbeing business founded by former Royal Marines Commandos Ben Williams and Antony Thompson: 'High-intensity projects, mismanaged quarters and objectives, with little rest between each, cause millions of employees to suffer exhaustion and burnout. And often, the only rest provided is annual leave, which is never enforced. So do this:'

1. Promote work–life balance. Ensure you prioritise wellbeing outside of work to prevent exhaustion – for example, exercise, walking, hobbies, family time, relationship investment, exploring passions, reading, art and so on.

2. At work, cultivate a supportive culture. Foster open communication, collaboration and empathy towards others; help others, even if it is only making someone a drink or asking how they are. A supportive work environment alleviates stress – no one achieves success purely on their own.

3. Ensure manageable workloads. Set realistic deadlines and regularly assess and adjust workloads to prevent becoming overwhelmed and to reduce stress and the risk of exhaustion.

4. Finally, listen to the warning signs. Act accordingly and attentively – often physical manifestations of stress are the body's way of telling us to come off the accelerator. Do it!

PRACTICAL APPLICATIONS

- Introspection, learning from past exhaustion and acknowledging 'personal triggers' while planning ahead to counter stress emergence, is absolutely fundamental to maintain performance and safeguard our wellbeing.

- Therefore, work hard to understand yourself during times of hardship and establish a solid and effective 'psychological monitoring skills' routine.

- We must learn how to turn the dial down, relax and be in the moment more. Planning strategic time away or leave and holiday periods is crucial. Do not leave it too late.

- Hard work matters, but so too does recovery. Having friends, family, hobbies and other escapes is vital for wellbeing and success. For instance, Nobel Prize-winning scientists are three times more likely than their scientific counterparts to have a hobby[10] … we need a break!

Phase Seven: Preventing Burnout

When the day came for me to travel to Manchester Airport, ready to fly out to Dubai and collect our Afghan visas, I met some of the lads on my contract, who were welcoming, and that settled me down slightly. The mind can be either your most powerful ally or your worst enemy; the battle between the two always lies within. For the past six weeks, it had tormented me beyond belief, convincing me that I would not return home from Afghanistan.

I can remember vividly getting breakfast in the Manchester departures area and looking across at a guy I had just met, thinking, you are going home after this and I'm not. I was feeling really conflicted about it. I could appreciate the thought was irrational, but I found it hard to discount at times. I would think it was a warning: my gut instinct telling me to abort and travel home. A glimmer of comfort came when I momentarily acknowledged the false truth, replacing it with positive affirmation and in-depth situational appraisal. However, this was exhausting and its engagement consumed my every minute.

Once in Dubai and with our Afghan visas in hand, we headed back to the airport the following morning, ready to depart for Kabul. I have flown to various locations around the world from the luxury of Dubai airport, but this time we were in the airport's 'armpit' terminal departure gate, where flights depart to the likes of Baghdad, Iran, Pakistan and Afghanistan. It was an unbelievable contrast to the plush, excessive financial trappings afforded by the main terminals.

The internal Middle Eastern terminal departures area had no recognisable food or drink restaurant brands, nor did it have any quality duty-free shops worth taking a look in. It was nothing short of a pure shit-hole – filthy and run down, with urinals full and overflowing with deep orange urine and faeces, sinks spilling over with dirty water, and in general stinking of wet dogs. As you can probably imagine, in terms of being environmentally restorative, this did absolutely nothing for my mental health.

Eventually we boarded and the reality of what I was embarking on hit me. I was sitting on a commercial flight about to take off to one of the most dangerous places on Earth. The flight would take about two hours and I spent most of it thinking how surreal it was that I was surrounded by people who may have wanted to kill me. I had the feeling of regret you can get when you board a massive rollercoaster, an overwhelming sensation the moment you are strapped in and begin to move but there is nothing you can do about it. You are going whether you like it or not.

The UK military send their troops for acclimatisation training in the run-up to deployments in the Middle East. Such training and 'environmentals' usually take place in Oman, where soldiers get used to the heat, climate and living conditions, while also undergoing intensive combat-ready training, which prepares them not only physically but, crucially, mentally too.

> Not on this occasion for me, though. Twenty-four hours earlier, I had been in the UK sitting in Nando's with my best mate. Now, within one hour, I was about to land in the most hostile environment in the world.

The landing was truly awful thanks to the altitude. Once we got through passport control and baggage collection, which was the most unwelcoming experience ever, we were abandoned in a sparse and lifeless arrivals terminal and informed via text to go and rendezvous with some of the in-country contract personnel in Carpark 3 (C3).

It was immediately apparent how unwelcoming it was at the airport and also how lawless and unorganised it all appeared. None of the airport staff wore uniforms: it felt like the Wild West. All of this fed into the anxiety you can experience during that initial exposure to this country, when coming from a Western culture. Even for me, a trained soldier who had spent several years in the Middle East, this was different. It was deeply unsettling and required all my mental resources to portray composure, despite dealing with the vulnerability I felt inside.

As we conversed with an obvious sense of unease, we stumbled upon a group of G4S lads who had also just arrived in the country. (G4S is the world's leading integrated security company, providing security solutions to governments, businesses and individuals in over 90 countries.) They told us it was 'dog shit' we had not been met by our company, as we now needed to catch an Afghani public airport bus to C3. We were not impressed, nor did we know where to go or who to trust, with the locals looking as if they wanted to gouge our eyes out.

Under coercive control from the locals, we boarded a bus with immense reluctance, verbally questioning our every action.

Meanwhile, a group of locals were fighting over who was going to load our baggage in return for a tip. At this stage, we didn't even know where the bus was going. It could quite easily have left the airport and headed into downtown Kabul.

The bus looked as if it had just been driven out of a scrapyard and yet again I embarked on a psychologically uncomfortable journey, sitting alongside a local man who kept begging for cash in return for unloading my luggage once the bus stopped. It was truly awful, claustrophobic, and I felt completely powerless. The bus finally stopped, quite randomly, and we were told to get off in an alleyway. Behind us was a distant view of the airport, and looking ahead down the alley we could see a crowd of locals, staring at us in a piercing manner. It was such an intense experience and we did not know which way to go. One of the lads and I wondered if we were being set up. There were five or six of us gathered by the step of the bus and collectively we asked, 'Right, what the **** is happening here?'

With limited options, we decided to venture down the alley towards the local waiting party and thankfully, after walking through the first wave of non-emotional locals, we saw two Western faces in body armour, wearing the TOR International logos on a small Velcro patch. (TOR is a leading risk management and training organisation promoting the health and safety of people worldwide.) What a relief!

After the brief meet and greet, we were led over to two white and silver armoured Toyota Land Cruisers, where another bunch of TOR lads were waiting for us. This initial encounter was less desirable, as the guys who had been in the country for a period before us began to establish alpha male status, swearing excessively, showing off and acting boisterously. It was bizarre and lacked both intelligence and bearing.

I had witnessed the same behaviour throughout my career in the Royal Marines and during the various roles I had undertaken in the private security sector. Experience had taught me that this was typically displayed by the weakest, those with low social intelligence and poor self-esteem. So I found this initial interaction quite interesting and observed it with interest as the weeks passed by.

As we travelled through Kabul, my senses were operating at full capacity – a mixture of fascination and anxious trepidation – as the project manager (PM) gave us the running commentary. It reminded me of being on an open-top, sightseeing bus trip driving around the London landmarks, only he was telling us about the various hits each passing location had taken over the past few weeks and months. These often involved Vehicle-borne Improvised Explosive Devices (VBIEDs), utilising cars, vans or tankers packed to the rafters with explosives and detonated via a suicide bomber, and directed at Western military or private security forces.

According to the PM, these took place mostly at key T- or four-way junctions in the city or on notorious roads like Jalalabad Road, with the occasional small-arms attacks being initiated from bridges. There had also been a recent trend of magnetic IEDs. These were often stuck to the side of armoured vehicles like ours while in traffic – which happened almost every time you left your base – by insurgents on bicycles or motorbikes.

So, despite being told at interview that 'Kabul was safer than walking the streets of London', it now appeared that such threat assessments were slightly inaccurate, to say the least.

At 5,900 feet above sea level, Kabul is situated in a narrow valley, wedged between the Hindu Kush mountains. The city was extremely hot and dusty and it made me feel immediately unwelcome, as if everyone and everything was hostile and against me. Out of all the unfavourable countries I had visited previously, this was a whole new beast entirely.

Operating here demanded sustained vigilance and used up most of my mental resources. There was very little green vegetation anywhere and what was visible was sparse, neglected and in desperate need of water. Signs of vandalism, smashed windows and abandoned buildings were prevalent on the streets of Kabul.

During the dark hours, a lack of street lighting cast the local villages into a thick, eerie darkness, which seemed to echo the piercing sounds of sporadic gun fire and wild dogs barking, growling and fighting.

By day, the Hindu Kush mountains with their snow-covered peaks drew my attention. This view gave me comfort and a feeling of solace, which made me think of home and my family. The illusion was often shattered by the sight of slaughtered animal carcasses piled high on the back of an old pick-up truck, with the head of a cow unceremoniously decorating the top of the pile.

After an anxious journey, we arrived at the TOR compound, which was situated off the Jalalabad Road. The nearest American camp was US Camp Phoenix, but should we have come under attack, we were aware that we were totally on our own.

The compound was stark, barren, run down and sparse – a far cry from what anyone would consider to be a secure location. The living quarters were made up of old shipping containers, in which the nineteen or so of us slept, washed and socialised. It was stripped of any Western homely comforts and represented a harsh, unforgiving environment, unbearably hot in the summer, which aggressively obliterated any of your sensual needs. It was also infested with rats and mice, and the flies were on another level. You simply could not escape them and during the summer months they swarmed upon us as if we were wild animals in Africa, attacking our eyes for moisture.

There was an oppressive sense of hostility and danger. In a very strange way, though, I found I was attracted to that. I wanted to experience the rawest form of war possible and I suppose this was fulfilling that need.

Within hours of arriving, we heard small-arms, AK-47 fire. At first it was some distance away and then it got closer and closer. To my surprise, none of the lads who were already living there had magazines loaded with ammunition, or in some cases even knew where their weapons were. Most of the weapons were kept in an armoury, which needed to be unlocked before we could take anything, but they did not have enough weapons for all of us. It was unbelievable in that kind of environment. Once the small-arms fire got uncomfortably close, lads were flapping and fighting over a box of old AK-47 rounds, trying frantically to push them into their magazines before taking up semi-defensive positions around the compound. I found this lack of preparation and their previous blasé approach to our dangerous location to be absolutely jaw-dropping.

This was not a direct attack on us, but it could easily have been the start of one and nobody was remotely prepared for it. If it had been a direct attack, undoubtedly we would have been killed. I had only been in the country for three hours.

Believe it or not, we did not have weapons movement licences to carry weapons in transit or in vehicles, but this did not stop us. After all, once you leave camp, how can you provide security or bodyguarding in Afghanistan without a firearm when everyone else is carrying weapons? Luckily the police never checked us, but if they had, we would have been arrested and that could have meant years in the Kabul prison, Pul-e-Charkhi.

After months of requests, we managed to get some weapons test-firing time on Camp Phoenix, where I discovered my weapon did not even work. I had been cutting around Afghanistan with a faulty gun. I was beyond frustrated, to say the least.

One thing I did find enlightening about my initial time in Afghanistan was that it was not as bad as I had projected while waiting to deploy. It was certainly hostile, but I had been here before to a certain extent. Now I had my feet on the ground, much of the anxiety I had experienced, the intrusive thoughts and the crippling stress, started to dissipate.

Unbelievably, I felt more uncomfortable and under threat waiting at home in the UK than I did now in Kabul. My mind had prepared me for an ultimate reality that was far worse than the actual experience. That Afghan scenario was nothing more than an illusion, although one that had pretty much destroyed me mentally, activating a constant and frightening state of cognitive burnout that brought me to my knees.

Airport runs

When the lads were returning from or going out on leave, we would do the airport run. This route was constantly patrolled by Taliban VBIEDs, who would drive between two significant roundabouts – one directly outside the airport – looking to attack Western forces or people coming in or out of the country.

The airport journey was always an anxious one. There was no way we would go unarmed, so we always carried pistols and concealed them under the seat or in our 'grab bags'. These were our lifelines and contained trauma medical kits, US flags, dollars up to 2K to buy our way out of certain situations, our passports to leave quickly if needed and other means of survival such as food and maps.

On one particular day, Neil had his pistol in the glove box and mine was in a concealed compartment in my grab bag. After leaving the compound and heading to the airport, we were stopped at gunpoint and pulled over by the NDS, the Afghan version of the American CIA or something similar. These guys were well trained but were seriously corrupt.

Two guys approached our vehicle with their AKs raised and shouting for us to open our doors. However, under no circumstances should you ever open your doors in transit, as you instantly lose your protection. We called it breaking the seal. They were grabbing the door handles and pulling so aggressively their hands were sliding off as they kept falling backwards, off balance, trying desperately to get us out. If I am perfectly honest, it was horrific. I could see it escalating to shots being fired and I did not fancy our chances at that point, with only pistols. All of a sudden, Neil pulled out a laminated ISAF

151

badge from the glove box, a badge that granted unrestricted coalition camp access, a kind of golden ticket that meant you were part of International Security Assistance Forces. To my surprise and relief, the two men lowered their weapons and drove off. That was one of many extremely twitchy experiences in Afghanistan.

Once back on the road and after a few more miles of pot-holed and heavily congested roads, the result of a socially unorganised and undisciplined driving culture, we arrived at the airport. We went through the first checkpoint with no problem and started queuing for the second and final checkpoint and passport control. Usually, we were waved straight through, but this time we could see an ANP (Afghan National Police) officer opening doors and searching vehicles. This was not a good sight and our anxiety escalated yet again to sky high after our previous roadside stop.

We were now one behind the car being searched and I knew our time was coming. They opened the driver's door and mine and started searching. The ANP policeman opened the glove box, the lid crashed onto my knees and Neil's pistol fell out. The guy grabbed it and erupted into a fit of blind rage. He began shouting and spitting at us in broken English, 'What is this? What is this?', while holding the pistol in my face and intoxicating me with his horrendous breath. After pointing the pistol in our direction, he stepped back, pulled back the slide, chambering a round, and to everyone's astonishment he pulled the trigger and fired a bullet into the floor. It went down through the crack of my bent left knee and under the vehicle. I was that close to being shot.

Immediately after this, the officer looked shocked, his face paled and he threw the loaded pistol into our vehicle while all the queuing locals fled, screaming and shouting like people reacting to gunfire in a Hollywood film.

By now, a wave of ANP officers was running towards us. I thought the policeman was going to say that I had tried to shoot him and they were coming to arrest us. For a moment it was terrifying, but when the officers arrived, they physically attacked their own guy, pushing him over the front of our vehicle before pulling his pants down and hitting him on the backside with their flip-flops. Then they screamed at us to leave. We drove off in shock and picked up the lads we had gone to collect.

This type of thing happened regularly in Afghanistan. Intensive, life-threatening situations came from literally nowhere and had the potential to go horribly wrong in a second, sensitive moments that hinged on a 50/50 split of luck and misfortune – life or death. An outcome we all treated as the somewhat comforting understanding that if your time is up, it's up. Therefore, why worry about it?

During my time in Afghanistan, I had a recurring dream. I had bought a house, you could say it was the house of my dreams. Only one room in the house had a severe drop in temperature the closer I got to it. The room was haunted and it scared me to death. Looking back, the house represented what should have been my 'safe place', yet it was not secure. An area of the house was not under my control and that correlated with my lived experience – the unknown and overwhelming uncertainty posed by Afghanistan and the lack of control I had in terms of my own mortality.

Lesson 7

Stress recovery

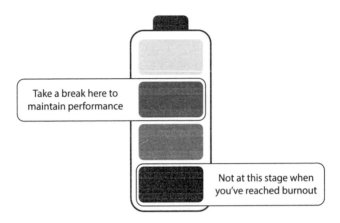

Figure 10.1 Your body battery

Before we delve in, to maintain cognitive performance it is essential to schedule planned/strategic rest during the maintenance of the behavioural alignment (performance) phase (see Figure 10.1). I appreciate that the above example of Afghanistan is extreme and very few will ever experience such circumstances, which would undoubtedly induce elements of stress in all of us. But I have experienced prolonged stress and the debilitating effects of burnout since then – in non-life-threatening circumstances – and the manifestations have been exactly the same as those I experienced while I was deployed in Afghanistan.

There is not only a significant relationship between burnout and depression,[1] but I believe all those who harness and utilise the growth mindset run a greater risk of experiencing such cognitive impairments.[2] Those who chase down success and push outside the comfort zone, taking on risks, discomfort and sacrifice by subscribing to the notion of delayed gratification, are increasingly more susceptible to the overlapping conditions of burnout and depression.

Dedication and focus take their toll after a period, which is often not helped by our tendency to fall victim to inattention blindness, a psychological occurrence that happens when we become so fixated on something that we neglect other aspects of our daily life, and in particular our wellbeing.[3] Therefore, via strategic goal acquisition preparation, you must factor in the mitigation of or recovery from burnout as an almost inevitable by-product of hunting down success and maintaining performance.

While depression is characterised by symptoms of low mood, anhedonia (*the inability to feel pleasure*), mental and physical fatigue and feelings of guilt, burnout is recognised as a three-dimensional syndrome involving physical and emotional exhaustion, sport or career devaluation, and a reduced sense of accomplishment.[4] Speaking personally, in the past I have experienced both cognitive inhibitors, but deciphering which is to blame for my impairment has been extremely difficult.

Although mental conditioning (*exposure*) can delay such conditions to some extent, we must arrive at the fundamental need to acknowledge the distinction between cognitive endurance and resilience, namely, that the continual application of resilience does not protect us against cognitive depletion (*burnout*). Therefore, we should think about resilience as cognitive endurance, which, like physical endurance, then invites us to acknowledge a phasing approach that is utilised in sport and competition to avoid 'over-training'.

Look at it like this: to maximise and maintain elite physical performance, we divide training into specific phases. For example:

*Accumulation (builds volume, aerobic work, movement effi-
ciency) > Intensity (enabled and weaponised by the quality of
the accumulation phase, this phase delivers top-end strength,
endurance, conditioning – delivering our performance at the
tip of the spear) > Peaking (game, event, competition-specific)
> Recovery and Reload*

Now, staying in 'intensity' will ultimately end in physical burnout. The trick for optimum physical endurance is to revisit
the accumulation phase and broaden the base further through
periodical rest, recovery and building, allowing you to peak for
longer the next time.

Yet, when it comes to the cognitive, we often go straight to
intensity and through the application of resilience, stay there
on full and relentless activation until we arrive at catastrophic
burnout. We are smarter than that for the physical application. Therefore, unless we apply a scientific and tailored mental endurance framework, we will never optimise our mental
capacity and elicit cognitive performance for longer. (Although
there is a catch, explored in the next chapter.)

A degree of resilience can help widen the extent to which we
can push for longer, but that is only prolonging the inevitable
relapse, and when it happens, we fall harder and deeper into
cognitive burnout. My point is that the mindset qualities we
all seek to accumulate, which fuel the constructs of success,
can produce side effects such as burnout and depression that
are only a switch away from debilitating us in our prime and
thus halting progress.

During the lead-up to and throughout my time in Afghanistan, I never thought I would get better: my head was like a
pressure cooker, with no room for thoughts or action. From the
outside, I was a former Royal Marines Commando, but inside

I felt that no words of encouragement or comfort could stop the way I was feeling. My identity not only pushed me forward, it entrapped me. However, during my leave periods and upon returning home for good, there was one thing I felt almost naturally inclined to do. There was one environmental setting that appeared to help my stress and recovery, one that has been 'scientifically proven' to restore our attentional resources and mitigate cognitive burnout.

Place and wellbeing

People rarely consider the place they are in to be connected to their wellbeing. Yet, according to Dr Roger Ulrich,[5] people find certain places to be psychologically restorative if they share similarities with the kind of natural landscapes in which humans evolved. In the past, I have worked in many hostile environments and upon my return to England, I have always been drawn to the Peak District. I have used this particular environment as a tool to reinvigorate myself after the dangerous and highly stressful working conditions of the Middle East.

According to Falk and Balling,[6] humans are known to show an innate preference for natural, savannah-type landscapes over urban settings, such as towns and cities, and may have innate sensory and perceptual systems better suited to these savannah-type settings.[7] Not only that, but humans have a visual sensitivity and preference for green light – specifically, the colour of chlorophyll (*plant pigmentation*) – adaptations that we acquired to distinguish between edible and poisonous leaves.[8]

For Stevenson[9] and Hartig et al.,[10] restorative environments have a positive effect on our wellbeing, reducing stress-related illness. They work to bring our functional resources back to baseline after they have been diminished through daily pressures, exhausting work commitments and stress.

To support this, in 1995, three experiments conducted by Stephan Kaplan[11] were designed to test the hypothesis that exposure to restorative environments enabled the recovery of mental fatigue. First, three groups of participants were mentally fatigued by performing a 'sustained attention test', then they were subjected to photographs of either restorative environments, non-restorative environments or geometrical patterns. Finally, they performed the sustained attention test again. Remarkably, or perhaps not, only participants exposed to the restorative environments improved their performance on the final attention test.

Ulrich's research findings[12] also support this, as patients with a natural view (as opposed to a view of a brick wall) 'needed to stay in hospital for a shorter time after their operation, took fewer painkillers, and received less negative evaluations'. Many other studies performed with different cultures of people have shown similar findings, including improved attention[13] and a more positive emotional state.[14]

PRACTICAL APPLICATIONS

- In general, we are unaware of the direct influence that environment has on our senses (positive or negative) and how, in turn, it impacts our wellbeing and performance outcomes.

- When it comes to achieving success, the selection of environment and the right social circles are crucial. They either harden you, facilitating emotional independence and preparing you for success, or soften you, setting up the ambush of failure.

- Upon returning from Afghanistan, the view of green fields from the aeroplane stimulated feelings of wellbeing, which may be explained by my predisposed connection to and reinforcement of the relaxing sensation I experience when in naturalistic environments. This reaction accounts for my preference for heading to the Peak District whenever I need to relax and achieve distraction.

- A Norwegian study[15] found that even the number of indoor plants near a worker's desk had a very small but statistically reliable association with reduced sick leave and increased productivity.

- Cognitive fatigue sabotages our aspirations and our hunger to continue. Therefore, for the benefit of our senses and attentional resources, and to assure successful outcomes for longer, we must seek exposure and better connection with the natural world.

- New beginnings require two fundamentals: the selection of environment and unique exposure(s), and incredible bravery to leave our comfort zone. Select wisely.

CHAPTER ELEVEN

Mental Health and Success

I have often found it difficult to convey the anti-climax of success to others. However, when forced to explore the experience more deeply while writing this book, I found the build-up to Christmas encapsulates it perfectly.

I have consistently felt lost and underwhelmed upon arriving at the finishing line and it is similar to the conflict many of us encounter as adults on Christmas Day. We fall in love with the magic of the festive period as it begins on the 1st of December and progresses to Christmas Eve. We are almost hypnotised by its seductive draw, riding the wave of fantasy as we spend, sacrifice and prepare for a wonderful Christmas Day. In a weird, psychological sense, we buy into the notion that not only can we create this magic, but somehow it will transform our daily lives, which to varying degrees are littered with financial woes, family issues and other external distractions. So, we invest hard in Christmas, believing it has the power to transport us to a place of divine happiness, even if it is only short term, while hoping that in some irrational way it will endure.

Ultimately, we arrive at Christmas Day in a place of psychological confusion. We know we should feel happy. After all, happiness is apparently everywhere. Yet inside we are conflicted and can feel incredibly let down on Christmas Day, as we realise it will not afford us the solace we were seeking. As a result, we descend mentally and emotionally into the New Year with work now visible on the horizon. We have been tricked by the fantasy of Christmas, and it will happen over and over again. However, all is not lost. It is not such a depressing reality if you are willing to change perspective.

The magic lies in the build-up, much like the journey towards goal acquisition. At the time, we are focused solely on the end result. As such, we are never fully in the moment and do not realise how good the build-up is until it is over. Christmas Day marks the end of that process, and let's face it, the end of anything good never delivers happiness.

Only recently have I come to understand this in relation to my own experiences of goal attainment. As I mentioned earlier, it is the journey I enjoy, rather than the sense of accomplishment upon completing it successfully. As soon as I achieve a personal goal, I experience a dip in mental wellbeing, often with some form of depression, and then instantly divert my attention to the next challenge to avoid the dip, in the hope of one day reaching fulfilment. However, this process has been exhausting and the method of approach has failed to address what is going on behind the curtain.

It is a potentially demoralising revelation, but it has allowed me to acknowledge that while I keep chasing the illusion of fulfilment, I will never be truly happy. Ultimate fulfilment never happens, and that is okay.

Coming to terms with this vital insight has brought me an air of peace, which has not stopped me from wanting to achieve but has allowed me to appreciate each day for all its ups and downs. It gives me the time to sit back, take in my surroundings and be present in the moment, instead of always being in some future tense.

This was not always so. During my twenties and early thirties, while armed with the shield of Royal Marines training and the subsequent spear of experience, I pushed on under the perceived cloak of resilience. I never understood that by engaging in a constant battle with life and goal acquisition, I would eventually compromise my armour. A reality that would gradually start to reveal the raw and unfiltered face of my own fragility.

One thing I do know is that from a very young age I have been embedded in tough, performance-demanding environments and without question all have expected and championed the 'stoic' elements of mindset application – for example, the need to endure pain and hardship without showing emotion or complaining. Now, such attributes are a necessity during game play in order to portray a lack of discomfort, fear or fatigue to an opposing team or competitor, or to an enemy in a military context. But to expect someone to maintain their sense of wellbeing behind the mask of this 'poker face' indefinitely goes against everything that it is to be human.

In the past, I have tried. I have taken the blueprint of what we believe constitutes resilience and applied it to all my ventures, whether in a military, private security or civilian world setting, both professionally and personally. This has ranged from renovating houses to living a life with discipline in order to be successful.

While such single-minded focus has often produced the end result, being so relentless until the task completion has produced unwanted side effects. The application of indefinite resilience, while having full confidence in my ability to complete a challenge or task, has always led to cognitive burnout. Back in 2017, for instance, I applied resilience to strengthen my determination to complete a major renovation of our former family home, at literally any cost. It ended in quite catastrophic financial issues.

OCD and chasing the stimulus

I have often wondered to what extent my OCD has played a part in this. It has completely shaped my life, demanding the elusive edge of perfection and keeping me ruthlessly consistent, and added the glue to the resilience enabling my successes. OCD facilitated the often stressful and exhausting daily urge to remain committed to tasks despite my setbacks. It energised the daily burden to keep a diary during my Royal Marines training, despite raw fatigue and exhaustion, rich content that went on to form the backbone of *Becoming the 0.1%*.

My OCD is still a daily battle, one that I have been frustratingly unable to conquer. It is a constant by-product of my exposures to adversity and the enduring responsibility of fatherhood. Depending on the day, it controls me and influences my behaviour, and at times, when I am particularly stressed, it consumes my existence. But it is not all bad.

Through a process of self-understanding and acceptance, I have chosen to embrace it. I like to see OCD as two sides of the same coin. It torments me relentlessly at times and creates a malfunction in the constructive evaluation of visual information and thus the world around me. But it is also what makes me incredibility effective when directing my attention towards achieving something long-term or complex. The question is, how many other people who achieve relative success do so fuelled by such mental issues? It is a reality we never consider or acknowledge.

In October 2023, UFC 294 took place in Abu Dhabi. The mixed martial arts event saw the UFC Featherweight World Champion, Alexander Volkanovski, step in at ten days' notice and move up a weight to face the formidable challenge of fighting the Khabib Nurmagomedov prodigy and reigning UFC Lightweight World Champion, Islam Makhachev. Although Alex lost for the second time – arguably expected given the mountain he had to climb at such short notice – it was what he said during his post-fight speech that I found fascinating:

> He is not somebody you should be taking a short-notice fight with, but I needed it. A lot of people will say it's for the money and all that, but it was much more than that, you know what I mean? It is hard, look, it really is hard for athletes … sorry, [he starts crying] oh, man … I never thought I would struggle with it, but for some reason when I wasn't fighting or in camp, I was just doing my head in. You know what I mean? I just needed a fight and this opportunity came up and I'll be honest, I wasn't training as much as I should have, but I thought I had to take it … I was struggling a little bit not fighting, I was doing my head in. Everything's fine, I've got a beautiful family – but I don't know, I think you just need to keep busy, so that's why I ask the UFC to keep me busy![1]

Like Alex – and this is only a recent observation – I understand that if my mind is fully engrossed in a journey towards achievement, I generally have good mental health and wellbeing. However, if my mind is not stimulated or tasked with repeated goal acquisition, I seem to fall out of cognitive balance and my mental health plummets.

I first became aware of this during university in my thirties. Throughout term time, I was under pressure and somewhat stressed, but in general I was in a good mental health. My mind was stimulated, I felt purposeful and engaged in aspiration. However, as soon as the study year finished, I started experiencing depression and stress, and as a result my anxiety and OCD got far worse.

So, while OCD and possibly elements of attention deficit hyperactivity disorder (ADHD) may have contributed to my success – affording me the ability to reload and go again, propelled by the fear of being average – each venture has ended in burnout and periodic bouts of depression. It got to the point where I could not even articulate properly. I became socially paranoid and therefore withdrawn. Once there, not only has recovery been a mountain to climb at times, but something else very powerful has restricted me from moving back up to full cognitive alignment, harmony and performance.

Masculinity and identity

My enduring quest for success and fulfilment required an ever-changing prescription of thinking and behaviour, which created a barrier of external expectation that was deeply oppressive. While financial responsibilities prevented me from slamming on the brakes during periods of mental health difficulties, especially throughout the nervous breakdown I suffered prior to deploying to Afghanistan, there was something else at play.

During dark times, there was an uncompromising internal need and external thirst to uphold the societal expectation of my identity: Gareth is a Royal Marine. This was extremely powerful.

In an attempt to uphold the construct of masculinity, while wearing the heavy cloak of resilience, I 'masked' – acted tough – and tried to hide the dire sense of vulnerability I was experiencing. I pretended to my family and to everyone I encountered that I was okay. In fact, I was struggling with my day-to-day commitments and pressures, a reality that was in dire conflict with my internal mechanisms. A problem, due to the socially archaic concept of masculinity whereby men are tough and do not display emotion, which entrapped me along with many other disproportionately affected men.

Certainly during my younger years, the need to uphold my perceived masculinity was so important that it was the biggest barrier to being able to express myself fully when I became ill. This made my harrowing existence even more incredibly lonely. After all, masculinity was the embodiment of my identity.

At the very heart of my reluctance to talk was a deep feeling of incompetence and the fear of being branded as mentally weak, the outcome of my career as a Royal Marines Commando and in hostile private security being too big for me to handle mentally. I did not want others to think I couldn't hack it or that the jobs had broken me.

Compounding things more, my skillset had pigeonholed me into niche job roles that demanded mental strength and maximum emotional control, such as hostile environment security work and bodyguarding. Going to the doctor and asking for help would have destroyed this avenue of work and income, as many companies demand a doctor's note of mental competency prior to someone being offered a job and possibly handling weapons. This would make everything I had done for ten years a complete waste of time. Therefore, I felt I had no option but to keep quiet, self-medicate with my mum's anti-depressants and 'crack on'.

In short, the need to live up to public expectation created a social barrier to speaking out, which trapped me even further in the vortex of burnout. This highlighted the classic public vs reality misconception, a conflict that is created between someone's personal viewpoint and what other people will expect from them, based on their profession and its associated construct of identity. This not only creates an unrealistic expectation from those 'outside the self', it can rapidly start to become unsustainable for the bearer.

So, what would I have done differently if I had been armed with greater self-understanding and the benefit of maturity? The short answer is … probably nothing. I do not believe my character and make-up would have allowed any deviation from the way I have executed my acquisition of success. I acknowledge that this is a by-product of being me. I must expect that cognitive exhaustion and burnout will lurk somewhere in the distant shadows, waiting to ambush me at any moment.

As a countermeasure, I have become better at identifying the triggers and have made a conscious effort to work in intervals, for example by alternating periods of deep work, sustained concentration and commitment to task, with periods of 'distracted' rest, such as gym training, walking, hobbies, richer family time, and reading or watching TV. Working on a ratio of 30–90-minute blocks of work, followed by 15–20 minutes' rest.

I recognise that this is often easier said than done. When I am feeling good – energised and motivated – I have often been mindful that my restless efforts will lead to exhaustion and burnout. But I have simply thought, I have been here before and I will crawl my way out of it again. However, once in the shadow of burnout, I have found the battle to re-establish cognitive stability and my overall wellbeing to be extremely challenging and, as a result, I have always vowed never to return.

One thing I do know is that success is ugly. It is painstaking, mundane, lonely and uncertain. And yet, remarkably addictive. While I would like to think we can arrive at the final destination with better overall wellbeing, being outside of our emotional comfort zone takes its toll, the pulls and stressors of which naturally drain our cognitive resources.

Reaching the end of any endeavour leaves battle scars.

Leave your comfort zone

By now, I hope you have begun to acknowledge the fluidity and the fragility of mindset: thinking, behavioural application and the need to establish healthy consistency.

Three years ago, when I mapped out the seven phases in this book, I did so because I felt I could have done things better to cushion my fall into burnout. Through my personal experience and the external perception of my identity, I wanted to reveal the true nature of how it feels to be 'inside the helmet'. By doing so, I hoped to arm the reader with a better understanding of how to maximise performance and safeguard our mental health.

So, how can we perform better for longer while upholding our mental wellbeing? Well, it is relatively simple in practice. But like all things in life that bring about significant change, it is the tiresome simplicity that kills the aspiration. As human beings, we appear to struggle with not achieving fast results. We want quick wins for our investment and sacrifice, and as a result we often display poor commitment to long-term personal ventures. Take weight loss, for instance, where instead of making minor adjustments and playing the long game, we crash diet, jump on the scales in a matter of days and if we haven't lost weight, we become disheartened and revert to our old ways. Very rarely do we make the fundamental changes that will formulate new lifestyles and subsequent opportunities.

We want instant fulfilment. Delayed gratification, where the riches lie in the future, doesn't work for us because we do not trust the process, but more importantly, we do not trust ourselves. So we opt for whatever we feel we are worth. In effect, we 'cash out' without holding it together to see the gamble pay off.

Long-term change is initiated the moment we decide to become the very best achievable versions of ourselves, underpinned by self-discipline where we subscribe to the notion of delayed gratification over cheap, quick and insubstantial pleasures. That is the moment when the detonating cord of success is ignited.

But as I have described earlier, the momentary euphoria that we experience when realising a personal milestone or achievement cannot be bottled. The output required to reach a significant goal often comes at the cost of our mental wellbeing. For the same qualities that facilitate tailored behaviour to ensure aspirational alignment also invite exhaustion and burnout if we fail to acknowledge the warning signs.

The holistic you

We add further value to our performance levels when we develop and incorporate our 'holistic person', a key element of performance that is often widely neglected. Becoming more holistic takes time; it is a process that is initiated by self-reflection and learning from past experiences – a fundamental understanding of yourself. Very rarely are we granted the controlled process of stress inoculation. More often, life sends the true test first and grants us the lesson afterwards, rich information that we rarely capitalise on through the lens of performance and wellbeing maintenance.

How do you start to become holistic and more well rounded? Look at it logically. In principle, it is about evaluating exactly where you are now and where you want to get to, while incorporating the finer details of past experiences. Imagine it is like going on a road trip, with yourself as the mode of transport. There are key elements of performance requirements that you will need to uphold if you are to arrive at your final destination efficiently. For example, it is essential to make sure the car is in good working condition. Before setting off, it is about planning routes, assessing the time to get there, fuelling up, checking oil and water, or buying drinks and snacks for the journey. On route, it involves stopping for petrol, getting refreshments or taking a rest.

During the journey, we remain aware of the vehicle and respond immediately to anything that does not feel right through corrective action, whether via our own hands or those of the roadside assistance. It is just that we don't do that when it comes to ourselves. In general, we ignore the warning signs. We proceed on and on under the false pretence of resilience, believing that it will transport us to our desired location. It can and it often does, but we arrive battered, bruised and often incapable of enjoying the spoils at the other end.

Much of this neglect is not intended. Due to the subjective nature of mindset, and the maintenance required to adapt successfully to external stimuli, it can become extremely difficult to mitigate the emergence of issues and provide adequate self-care, until it is too late. That is why reflection-led introspection is so important. Keeping mindset finely tuned, balanced and in sync with a particular endeavour can frequently elicit the emergence of stress and exhaustion. Usually, at that point, if we are not careful and attentive, the wellbeing ship sets sail and a period of recovery is required.

When extreme stress strikes and lingers, opening the door to possible burnout, shift action is essential, informed by holistic understandings. Three symptoms characterise burnout: exhaustion, cynicism or distancing, and feelings of incompetence or lack of achievement. Research has linked burnout to many health problems, including hypertension, sleep disturbances, depression and substance abuse.[2]

There are immediate actions you can take:

1. Address self-care. This is often neglected prior to and during burnout. Write down areas that could be improved to facilitate better feelings of self-esteem.

2. Shift perspective to determine which aspects of your situation are fixed or can be changed. Give yourself one to two weeks to benefit from your lifestyle adjustments.

3. Reduce exposure to the most stressful activities and relationships. Rate each on a scale of one to ten, where one equals angry, frustrated or drained and ten equals joyful and relaxed.

4. Seek out helpful interpersonal connections. People who are not essential, or who put you in a negative mood, must go.

Once you reach this stage, the investment in self-care is essential. The key is to replenish your physical and emotional energy, along with your capacity to focus, known as your attentional resources. This is expedited through prioritising good sleep habits, which often require immense discipline, better nutrition, regular exercise and seeking beneficial social connections.

Wellbeing practices such as reading, journalling and exposure to and enjoying nature[3] can also replenish and rebalance the nervous system. If the basic principle of restoration is to disconnect and replenish your attentional resources to counter stress and the emergence of burnout, then the natural world 'restorative environments' can provide the very best cognitive medication.

The resilience paradox

However, there is a paradox in relation to resilience and the cultivation of mental toughness, which we must acknowledge as a precursor to potential mental health issues.

A science-based approach and subsequent understanding used to formulate a preventive burnout framework, built into elite environments or even our daily routines, could prevent cognitive exhaustion and catastrophic burnout through management and mitigation. For certain jobs, such as professional sporting athletes and those serving in the military, science would undoubtedly restrict the depths that are required to take an individual mentally in order to cultivate the skillset needed to achieve extraordinary feats of human performance. Taking a timid and uninitiated young adult, for example, and exposing them to Royal Marines Commando Training, before injecting them into war zones and conflict. Science and ethical standards would hinder this process and have negative consequences.

Although contemporary science rightly has a valuable place in many sporting environments and beyond, I believe that restricting mental hardship and suffering in practice, while still trying to achieve mental resilience, would be detrimental to producing the fortitude required to be effective in some occupations and arenas. Perhaps we have to accept that the degrees of mental health issues that follow elite-level professions are not only a by-product of cultivating resilience-based human engineering. They are a necessary evil that we must acknowledge and also invest in when piecing someone back together once their work is done.

Our perception of mentally tough people creates a barrier for growth that emerges from the very heart of the paradox. Not only does this maintain the facade and the rigid expectation of resilience, but the high pedestal on which we place those people seems beyond our reach. As a consequence, we never feel ready to pursue our dreams or fully realise our potential.

Our misplaced understanding of the construct of resilience means that we believe those who repeatedly achieve great things do so because they were born resilient. They travel through life unaffected by the everyday pressures that affect us all. This is simply not true. On the contrary, resilience constructs barriers everywhere to conceal the fact that it is an illusionist, an imposter to growth, mental health and wellbeing.

We are all human, and what affects one, affects the other to a certain degree. Under pressure, stress and adversity, we all have that inner voice that tells us how to find the unceremonious exit. Failing to acknowledge this only adds to the belief that we are not ready or good enough to step outside the comfort zone and maximise our potential, based on feelings of incompetence or emotional bearing. This illusion needs to be overcome. *All* people experience the same emotional responses. The secret is that those who constantly expose themselves to adversity learn how to manage their emotional responses and thus, by default, find more success.

Societal pressure plays a huge role in shaping our behaviour. It affects how we evaluate risk and what actions we take. It coerces us into investing time in false materialistic values and assets over personal relationships, which often manifests in the neglect of family time and experiences. Catastrophically, it restricts our ability to speak out when we enter the darkness or, conversely, how we perceive others fighting their own battles.

Pursuing happiness and fulfilment through an ideal of achievement, amassed wealth or social status can also have a crushing impact on mental health. This perceived notion of finding happiness through success and wealth confuses the spectator whenever a sporting icon speaks out to say they are suffering with depression, while it continues to entrap people in a cycle of flawed belief. The whole construct is a dangerous illusion that neglects all other aspects of our lives and, more importantly, our emotional regulation.

As human beings, we are influenced by society to chase the wrong objectives to establish happiness, which go against our evolutionary emotional needs. We chase money, often to the detriment of quality time with our loved ones, and only seem to realise when it is too late, the kids have got older or the partner has left.

The big question we need to ask ourselves is whether we are present to enjoy the moment or are we guilty of living in a permanent state of future projection, believing that everything we desire is at some 'final destination'? One we never actually realise.

Hopefully, you are now reflecting on your own existence and considering how you can engage with the world around you, armed with a greater understanding of how mindset works. Whether we are born with a mindset preprogrammed or we acquire it during childhood and early adulthood experiences is a debate that will endure for decades. What I do know, based on my own experiences, is that our mindset is adaptable, fluid and susceptible. It is somewhat fragile and thus it requires constant self-care and attention. But it can be conditioned to deliver the results you desire – of that I have no doubt at all.

The Interviews

During the compilation of this book, I had the privilege to speak to various elite athletes, coaches and former military operators. I wanted to discover their personal experiences of maintaining performance, how they delivered consistent behaviour and whether elements of mental health underpinned it. In particular I was curious as to how they facilitated the one-percenters to retain goal-orientated alignment, thus enabling them to reach the top of their chosen field. Also of interest was the potential detrimental impact that their chosen professions had on their wellbeing or personal lives, and their ability to remain on the rails and stay focused, and how they coped mentally and physically with change and transition.

Jamie Peacock MBE: former GB Lions and England rugby league captain

Jamie Peacock is one of the most decorated players in rugby league history. He is a former Bradford Bulls, Leeds Rhinos and GB Lions and England rugby league captain and won nine Grand Finals while at Bradford and Leeds. Since retiring from the sport as a player in 2015, he has become a motivational speaker and leadership mentor.

How do you maintain performance and what underpins it?
I developed consistent performance as I gained experience. As I got 250–300 professional games in, I knew what I needed to do and how my output had the best effect on the team. I focused on the deliverables and was less focused on outside thoughts and opinions. [I was] just more interested in my internal thoughts and what I could control.

From an outside perspective, I read books or watch inspirational programmes to influence or top up my motivation. Also, if someone tells me I can't do something, I use it to drive me forward, to weaponise the outside influences and motivate me internally. 'Pissed-off people change the world!' Right?

I guess my main motivation for wanting to maintain performance was always trying to be excellent. I enjoyed being considered excellent. I relished being on that type of pedestal and I wanted to live up to that expectation by the lads [*teammates*].

How do you maintain behavioural alignment towards a goal?
Set a goal and hold yourself accountable. You need to look in the mirror and see yourself. Are you achieving that goal? You must deliver on what you set or you let yourself or the team down. Also, intrinsic day-to-day goals are key: the standards to which you hold yourself. Just being excellent at whatever you do. Yeah, just striving to be excellent. I hold myself accountable every day.

What negative mental factors have you encountered from trying to maintain performance and alignment?
Adhering to high standards brings a lot of internal stress. No one is bullet-proof. Some days I wake up and I really don't feel excellent or motivated. When I played, that brought me a lot of stress.

People put you on pedestal, which naturally brings pressure, and sometimes you want to turn that pressure off. Some days, it's about winning the battle with that inner voice. I want to tell that inner voice to just switch off, especially when I was playing. Yeah, the weight of [external] pressure based on expectation, this can make you not enjoy it.

The toughest part in trying to be resilient was when my dad died and I had to keep playing. I found it hard to remain resilient then. I have, however, become more realistic about things now. For example, during my twenties, I think the passing of my dad would have destroyed me, but as I've gotten older, I've become chilled with it. More chilled in myself.

Shaunie Gwen-Gibson: Hyrox world championship competitor

Shaunie Gwen-Gibson battled anorexia and thus decided to dedicate her time to the study, understanding and importance of mental health and wellbeing, and the integration of women's performance in sport from a mindset perspective. Utilising such learning and applications, Shaunie has become a world championship competitor in the indoor fitness sport of Hyrox and now coaches others in taking control of their wellbeing through mindset practices.

How do you maintain performance and what underpins it?
Purpose and potential. Understanding my 'purpose' is critical to allow me to apply myself and keep me driven to reach my full potential. For me [mentally], this is a drive to be better than I was yesterday, to continuously seek improvement and to maximise my full potential. I will never forget a lesson from my dad when I was struggling to complete an

art assignment at college: 'You can do whatever you set your mind to.' I truly believe this and that is why I will never stop trying.

Externally, my purpose is driven by the people I am surrounded by and they are key to my success. My coach will often explain my purpose for the next six-week training block, as an example. Therefore, I am clear on my purpose for the next six-week cycle and I know exactly where I need to place my focus and energy. Other external factors include making my family proud, as family is a key value of mine, and something which I have always harnessed to help me tackle challenges to reach my goals.

How do you maintain behavioural alignment towards a goal?
Consistency! Embedding it into my daily routine. Without it, I don't feel like I am fulfilling my purpose, potential and authentic self. Being consistent in my behaviours around sleep, nutrition, mindfulness practices and training application is key to my success. For example, when it comes to sleeping, I ensure my technology devices are on sleep mode from 9.30 p.m. onwards and out of the room. This allows me to wind down before bed and improves my sleep performance.

Commitment and dedication are high personal values that have been embedded in me from a young age. These characteristics are also embedded into my behaviours. If I am not fully committed or dedicated to the cause, how can I expect to succeed? For me, daily routines inform a structured process that allows me to see my progress via data-driven results. When work gets in the way and disrupts my routine, then I accept this and replan to adapt to this change.

Does your previous eating disorder maintain your behavioural alignment in relation to performance?

I guess it does. Or at least, it has definitely got an underlying foundation. Any eating disorder has a significant obsessive element, which I have weaponised to push me to improve and constantly get better. In the past, performance was fuelled by obsession and it was unhealthy. Now, with time, it is more fuelled by a motivation to get better and to be successful in my sport, Hyrox. Now it's a want rather than a must, I have a much healthier relationship around sport and competition.

I still struggle with all the things I used to struggle with during my eating disorder, like calorie control, and sometimes that leads to under-fuelling. Which obviously has a negative impact on my performance. So for me, I am often trying to find the right balance between old habits and new motivations and a need to uphold performance and improve as an athlete. I have good days and bad days – it's a process!

What negative mental factors have you encountered from trying to maintain performance and alignment?

Questioning that purpose and potential. It can become tough to continuously push your mental and physical boundaries and make the required sacrifices to reach your goals. Sometimes this does lead you to question why you do this and if you can actually do this. 'Do I have that potential?' 'Do I actually want this?' I normally then have to remind myself that these days will come and I refocus on why I choose to maintain performance: my end goal and the idea of not meeting my full potential.

Do you find such cognitive distortions to be an opportunity or a hindrance to preserving consistency?

An opportunity, definitely. Consistency has been built and also resilience. I have constantly had to fight negative thoughts to get to where I want to be, so it has all been an extra challenge that I've had to overcome. Because of that, no matter what I face in life now, I feel equipped to overcome anything. I am not scared of change because I know I can adapt and thrive. Therefore, I see things as an opportunity rather than a hindrance. I have not only built my body to perform over time but also my mind.

Liam Harrison: eight-times World Thai Boxing champion

With eight world titles and a record of 115 fights with 87 wins and 48 by knockout, Liam Harrison has been number one in the UK rankings since the age of seventeen. He is widely regarded as the best Muay Thai fighter ever to come out of the UK.

How do you maintain performance and what underpins it?

For me, it is simple, it comes down to 'why': why you are doing it, what you are striving for. What is the why? Mine is serious. I once wanted to fight all the best guys in the world, to have the belts. In recent years, however, my why has changed; now I want to be remembered for being the most entertaining fighter who was in the most entertaining fights. When people look back and remember me, I want them to remember me as a savage!

How do you maintain behavioural alignment towards a goal?

I keep coming back to the why. If I fancy a night out, eating crap, having beer, I think back to my why and that keeps me locked in and focused. In my game, someone is always trying harder to beat you in all aspects of training – diet, cardio, strength and conditioning – but I cannot give anyone that edge on me, as there is no margin for error.

My favourite quote is: 'Success is not owned, it's rented, and the rent is due every day.' There is always someone training harder and everyone can get 1 per cent better each day.

What negative mental factors have you encountered or experienced from trying to maintain performance and alignment?
Without me being goal-focused mentally or if the stimulus is removed, things go negative. My energy gets channelled into destructive behaviours. Luckily, I have massive support from my partner Kate and my mum, dad and family.

Vicky Fleetwood: England rugby union player and Women's World Cup winner

Vicky Fleetwood is a woman of many talents. In her younger days, she was a junior hurdler before making the transition to rugby union. Vicky has reached the very highest level of the game, playing for Saracens and representing England, winning 82 caps and being an integral part of the Women's Rugby World Cup-winning team in 2014. Subsequently, she was also part of England's bronze medal-winning sevens squad in the 2018 Commonwealth Games on Australia's Gold Coast.

After her recent retirement from the game, she has now gone into coaching, while providing personal training on the side, and has since filled the void of playing rugby with a keen interest and participation in the sport of CrossFit.

How do you maintain performance and what underpins it?

The correct mindset is key, but once you have got it, it doesn't stay. You have got to be honest with yourself: it is easy to do the things you are good at, but not so the things you are weak at – people really need to practise their weaknesses.

Feedback is key to getting better and performing and you should always be prepared to take it, good or bad. Personally, if I am not good at something, I'm not happy – but I actually enjoy this! I enjoy not being good because it provides an opportunity to work on it and get better. I enjoy the challenge of getting better at something, something that intrigues me.

I have recently jumped into CrossFit and improving skills I was not good at has been the test I needed post-rugby. I feel like I reached the ceiling in terms of my rugby career, but taking up CrossFit seems to have filled the void I needed for competition, and being around like-minded people certainly helps me. For me, I am always trying to improve, that's daily, and improving on my weakness is key to maintaining performance.

How do you maintain behavioural alignment towards a goal?

Again, it is about being honest with yourself and trusting the process. For example, if my goal is by next year I want to be competing at the CrossFit Games, right now that is not going to happen. It is about making sure goals are attainable first.

You have to know yourself, listen to your body and understand your mind. Even when I was playing, there were times when I felt good and times when I felt my body was wrecked. I have never struggled with motivation – even if I felt like crap, something within forces me to go and do what I don't want to do.

I have questioned this recently and brought it up with Vicky. I believe motivation does go, but by embedding certain habits over long periods of time, they eventually become innate behaviours.

Once this happens, these innate behaviours provide a 'fail safe' to maintain behavioural enactment. For example, the upkeep of self-discipline, which in turn facilitates the establishment of solid routines. Those routines that are not always comforting but which produce successful outcomes will remain when motivation temporarily subsides.

Delayed gratification practised daily, like not sitting down in the gym or going on your mobile between sets, listening to music during running, or resisting dessert when someone hands you the dessert menu, all this builds resilience. So does undertaking exercise when you don't necessarily feel like it and not making excuses – these are all examples of how to maintain such behaviours and habitual routines.

What forces you out, is it an urge or a feeling of personal guilt?
I feel that if I don't do it, I will feel crap mentally. I don't want to miss out on the endorphins because that feels better than not doing anything. So, going out to the gym when I don't want to is a major internal conflict. However, once I'm there and afterwards, I always feel better after doing it. Don't get me wrong, I don't always go and 'send it' [*give it her all*], but just going through the motions and being around like-minded people really helps sometimes to lift me up and transform my state of mind.

What negative mental factors have you encountered from trying to maintain performance and alignment?
Well, recently I have worked on the mindfulness, wellbeing side. I always feel I can be 1 per cent better, but there are just not enough hours in the day to improve and get better, and because of that, I am high-anxiety. I think that is why I have been so successful. I do, however, find it hard to switch off and relax.

I need to avoid abject failure. Internally and externally, I don't want to be perceived to be crap. I had a twin brother, so that is maybe a factor in all this competitiveness. My twin brother was naturally more gifted at sports, so I have always had to work harder to get the better of him. As a result, I have always had trouble sleeping. Then I get stressed when I can't sleep. Once before an international game, I got only one hour's sleep! I went to see the doctor and he said, 'It's the sleep *before* that is key and will carry you through.'

The more I hear about ADHD and look into it, the more I become intrigued, as I can never sit still. My resting heart rate is higher than normal and I am naturally anxious. This was discovered through analytics, by taking my resting heart rate at England. Mine was fifty-four [beats per minute], which, for an elite athlete, is super high, given I was one of the fittest on the team. My mind is always active. I am always stressed, always driving away from home and going through a mental tick list.

What are your personal bugbears?
I hate people being late, hate excuses. I have no time for people that say they can't find the time to train, for instance. I can't stand people not being on point and if you say you are going to do something, do it! And don't make excuses. However, having this mindset is a trade-off. Yes, we get stuff done, but we also think in more detail than most people and I think it has far-reaching [negative] consequences.

I too slept for only one hour prior to undertaking the 30-miler on the final Commando Test and Kev Sinfield, an England rugby union coach, struggled to sleep both before and during his '7 in 7 Challenge' (seven marathons in seven days) for his former team-mate, Rob Burrow. This is often something the spectator doesn't realise: the sheer grit and personal resolve required to step out of one's comfort zone, to go against every physical and mental barrier and perform, despite such debilitating factors as a lack of sleep.

I can remember lying in bed, thinking I had no option, 'so sod it, what will be will be, shit or bust, I will be there at the end no matter what it takes.' For Kev, he made his sleeping difficulties a part of the challenge.

When you strip it all back, do you know what it comes down to in all these cases? Acceptance. Nothing in life goes to plan. In the Royal Marines, we have a saying, 'No plan survives the first contact', meaning the first enemy engagement or adverse outcome. Everyday life is no different. Shit happens and 'mental adaptivity' is fundamental to maintaining success.

Chris Oliver: former Royal Marines Commando mountain leader, UKSF operator and current Channel 4 *SAS Who Dares Wins* directing staff

Chris Oliver joined the Royal Marines at sixteen years of age. He subsequently completed the Royal Marines Mountain Leader (ML) course during his nine years of service in the Royal Marines, a course widely regarded as the hardest and most respected specialisation within the Royal Marines. Chris later went on UKSF Selection along with another 279 military personnel and was one of only twenty-two 'badged' [*successful*] for the SAS or SBS combined. He later specialised in 'Mountain Troop' within the Special Boat Service. With seventeen years' military experience, Chris has deployed on elite military operations in Sierra Leone, Northern Ireland, Iraq and Afghanistan.

How do you maintain performance and what underpins it?

It is a strange one, when you're competing within a group yet it is down to you and you alone to pass the course [*Commando Training/UKSF Selection*]. You don't know or feel any different from the rest; everyone appears to be at the same standard. It is not until people start dropping out that you question things, you start to think, hang on a minute, I still feel good, physically and mentally strong.

It is weird, me and Foxy [*Jason Fox: former UKSF operator*] have spoken about this recently, when someone drops out or VWs [*voluntary withdrawals*], it is like you steal their power, it empowers you to continue. It gives you that boost, that self-confidence to continue. Foxy says it's like the film *Highlander*: you take their power and become stronger, even more powerful mentally.

That is why it is so important to identify and surround yourself with like-minded people who want to go on that journey. They provide the safety net, it is safety in numbers, right?

How did you maintain behavioural alignment towards your goal during selection for the Special Boat Service?

Process, trusting the process: 'Keep turning rations to poo.' Focus on the process, getting from A to B, look at what's involved, how do you get there and then go all in: 'I put all my shit in one sock.'

In his first answer, Chris means just to be there every day, keep turning up and eat what you're given, then turn it to poo. In very simplistic terms, that is all you have to do. Take away the complexity, don't look beyond each day and keep doing the basics.

The second part is all about being fully organised and mentally prepared. Having to 'use two socks for one poo' is considered wasteful, therefore the term refers to a productive use of available resources, being efficient with time and focusing one's energy on a singular endeavour.

How did just twenty-two candidates find success out of 280 already serving and seasoned military personnel? What did you possess that the others did not?

For years, I thought, are we special [*special needs*], is something missing, or are we just 'solid' [*intellectually challenged*]? But no, over the years I have realised we are more adaptable and flexible in thought, which enables us to overcome adversity – I mean some of it was leaping [*horrific*] – and not to deviate from the plan and reach the goal, no matter what. Yes, I enjoy a drink and having fun, but in moderation: one eye is always on what I need to do to achieve what I need to achieve.

For the 258 that failed selection, what were the three main saboteurs to their endeavour?

Firstly, people turned up to the course with basically an opinion, a vision of what they thought of the Special Forces. A little bit like when they join the Royal Marines, they want to be a Marine, but they massively underestimate the hard work it is going to entail. So as soon as it started getting cold, wet and miserable and they needed to harness the resilience to do that every day, they didn't want it. They found an excuse to get out of there. That was one group of people – the majority!

Secondly, there were some people who physically couldn't do it, which was a minority to be honest. People were generally fit enough, but again, they could not harness the fortitude to do it day in, day out. This group represented about 5–10 per cent.

Thirdly, again this was a small amount of people, probably 15–20 per cent, when we started getting more technical on the course, i.e. the learning curve, which is steep, they couldn't keep up with it. They didn't have the ability to process the information quick enough. We would get shown something, a bit like the Royal Marines, and it is fine not getting it the first time, but when you start making mistakes, that's when it becomes a problem. There's just not the time to keep revisiting it, so they would get pulled, whether that was for safety on the ranges or just not able to absorb the information under fatigue.

Chris added that nearly all those who left were there for the wrong reasons. Barring genuine injury, around 60 per cent of those that failed were mentally underprepared or had not fully acknowledged the sacrifice required. They were mentally weak and thought of a million and one excuses to withdraw, almost convincing themselves in their own minds.

Every morning the DS (directing staff) asked, 'Does anyone not want to be here, anyone wanna leave?' And people would put their hands up to leave and I was laughing, thinking, I've been on harder exercises on Barry Buddon, in Scotland!

What prevented you from putting your hand up?

It comes down to preparation and also understanding your value and the stock that you come from [*Royal Marines*]. I was quietly confident going into it. My preparation was good: I had done the Royal Marines, I had done the ML [*Mountain Leader course*], I had done my jungle warfare course. So I knew going into it that if *I* was going to fail, then a lot of people would.

I totally believe that if you are confident in your own ability, you have invested in the right mindset and your physical preparation has been correct, we can all meet that standard. 'Mentally adaptable' is the key: self-regulation and self-reflection. Analyse yourself. Are you giving enough? Second-guess yourself, ask yourself questions, so that you understand where you are mentally but, more so, on the course.

In short, mental preparation is key and making sure your physical is up to standard, that your personal admin is on point, and your family life is in order. You want no distractions whatsoever that give you reasons to leave. Your 'why' has to be strong.

What negative mental factors have you encountered from trying to maintain performance and alignment?

From a mental perspective, I think the military sometimes get it massively wrong. For me, it is about picking your battles. Applying resilience to everything and in every situation doesn't always help and can lead to getting burnt out [mentally]. The military are really bad at that. Mental adaptability is key.

In summary

What I found fascinating during and after this process of interviewing was that those exceptional individuals above had all uncovered their purpose in life, an intrinsic passion, a calling they had made deeply personal and as such, the implementation of daily routine and non-negotiable commitments had been vital to securing success. Yet the upkeep of such behaviours to facilitate sustained performance was not only a daily commitment but often a conflicting battle.

That said, despite the daily distractions and obstacles none of us can evade – work commitments, injury or illness, travel, having or managing children, relationship problems – none of them strayed from the behaviours that maintained alignment to their goals or careers. They made daily adaptations, remained flexible in thought and made sure their behavioural success fundamentals were met, which sometimes went against their natural instincts. Just like all high achievers, they had become exceptional at delayed gratification.

Ultimately, discovering their purpose and harnessing the courage to pursue their goal not only required a strategic approach, it needed a strong stimulus to maintain behaviour in spite of adversity. The words 'process' and 'adaptability', meaning acceptance, were inherent in nearly all the interviews.

Most mentioned the underlying requirement to trust the process, the mundane nature of living and executing their day-to-day schedules with self-discipline. This meant repeating the same strategic behaviours over and over, staying committed and adaptive to daily unforeseen and uncontrollable change. A benefit only afforded to those who had stepped outside of their comfort zone at some stage during their lives and overcome various obstacles and adversity. Along the way, they had gained the knowledge that behavioural consistency and perseverance always trumped adversity and setbacks.

What was strikingly evident was the fact they all acknowledged that distractions were ever present and ready to derail their behavioural alignment. Liam came back to his 'why' to keep him 'on the rails'; for Chris, it was an understanding that moderation was key, again underpinned by a subconscious connection to his why. Shaunie came back to 'her purpose' and Vicky alluded to inner feelings of emotional guilt, desperately not wanting to let herself down, despite days when she did not want to do a particular training session.

There was emotional conflict embedded in the psychology of each interview, but solid behavioural foundations had been established and adapted over years to promote successful outcomes in light of change, even if, like Vicky (and myself), that came at the detriment of mental health and wellbeing. Obsession can be both a gift and a curse.

Your 'why' is your purpose – a calling. You have got to make it deeply personal, an entanglement of love and hate. Let it stir your soul and make you emotional. Let the magnitude of it scare you to death, make you angry and fearful, and thus get aggressive with it. Allow it to infect every fibre of your psychology!

Acknowledgements

I would like to take this opportunity to thank my literary agent, Nick Walters. Thank you, Nick, for always representing my work, supporting and believing in me. Thanks again for your vision and advice for *Becoming the 0.1%* and helping to bring that project to life, as well as bearing with me during the formation of this book during the pitching phase. It is always a great pleasure and a genuine privilege to be on this journey with you, someone I can now call a friend.

To Holly Bennion, my editorial director at NB Publishing. Thank you so much for seeing the potential in this project and for sharing my vision for it. Holly, it has been a pleasure working with you and meeting to discuss and explore the potential of this book. Thank you for believing in me and sharing my ambitions for the Academy.

To Barry Johnston, my copyeditor on *Becoming the 0.1%* and on this project. Barry, I cannot begin to express how grateful I am for the influence you have had on my works to date. It is such a rare and unique privilege to find someone who shares and imparts the same energy for my work as I do. I greatly appreciate you, Barry, and I value our collaborations and working relationship immensely. Hopefully many more to come!

To my darling boy, Jax, the driving force behind me and the one thing that keeps me dedicated to producing excellence when motivation strays. I absolutely adore you, son. You are my world and in time I hope my work inspires you to be a better man and chase down your dreams.

To Ann Hopton, very much my university mentor. Thank you, Ann, for all your unconditional support and for helping me (sometimes dragging me) through my studies. Thank you for challenging me to think critically, step outside of my comfort zone and become a better writer. I will always treasure the journey with your support while acknowledging your fundamental impact on where I find myself today. Thank you, Ann!

Thanks to Alexei Janssen for kindly allowing me to share snippets of his content and to capitalise on his observations. Alexei, I could have talked to you for hours on the topic of innate ability, performance and success outcomes. I found it completely fascinating (see www.alexei.co.uk).

I also want to dedicate a huge thanks to Vicky Fleetwood, Shaunie Gwen-Gibson, Liam Harrison, Chris Oliver, Jamie Peacock MBE and Dr Stuart Wilkinson. Thank you so much for agreeing to talk with me about your experiences and insights and for sharing such fantastic wisdom in relation to performance and your interpretation of success. Your time, openness and willingness to contribute have been greatly appreciated.

Source Notes

CHAPTER 1 THE MISCONCEPTION OF ELITE MINDSETS

1 https://www.dailymail.co.uk/news/article-9835069/PIERS-MORGAN-Sorry-Simone-boast-GOAT-selfishly-quit.html

2 Festinger, L. (1954). 'A theory of social comparison processes', *Human Relations*, 7(2), pp. 117–40. https://journals.sagepub.com/doi/abs/10.1177/001872675400700202

CHAPTER 2 MINDSET DEVELOPMENT AND ABILITY

1 Arlinghaus, K.R. and Johnston, C.A. (2018). 'The importance of creating habits and routine', *Am J Lifestyle Med.*, 13(2), pp. 142–4. doi: 10.1177/1559827618818044. PMID: 30800018; PMCID: PMC6378489

2 Deary, I.J. (2001). 'Human intelligence differences: A recent history', *Trends in Cognitive Sciences*, 5(3), pp. 127–30.

3 Ashbury, K. and Plomin, R. (2013). *G is for Genes: The Impact of Genetics on Education and Achievement*, John Wiley & Sons, Chichester.

4 Nisbett, R.E., Aronson, J., Blair, C., Dickens, W., Flynn, J., Halpern, D.F. and Turkheimer, E. (2012). 'Intelligence: New findings and theoretical developments', *Am Psychol.*, 67(2), pp. 130–59. doi: 10.1037/a0026699; Epub 2 January 2012. Erratum in: *Am Psychol.*, February 2012, 67(2), p. 129. PMID: 22233090.

5 Joseph, J. (2013). 'The lost study: A 1998 adoption study of personality that found no genetic relationship between birth-parents and their 240 adopted-away biological offspring', Private Practice, Clinical Psychology, Oakland, CA, USA. https://gwern.net/doc/genetics/heritable/adoption/2013-joseph.pdf

6 Richardson, K. (1998). *The Origins of Human Potential: Evolution, development and psychology*, Routledge, London.

7 Gladwell, M. (2008). *Outliers: The Story of Success*, Little, Brown, London.

8 Ericsson, K.A., Krampe, R.T. and Tesch-Römer, C. (1993). 'The role of deliberate practice in the acquisition of expert performance', *Psychological Review*, 100(3), pp. 363–406.

9 Gladwell, *Outliers*.

10 Ibid.

11 Ibid.

CHAPTER 3 THE REALITY OF MINDSET

1 Timmins, G. (2021). *Becoming the 0.1%: Thirty-four lessons from the diary of a Royal Marines Commando recruit*, Hodder and Stoughton, London.

CHAPTER 4 PHASE ONE: CULTIVATING MENTAL TOUGHNESS

1 McAdams, D.P. and McLean, K.C. (2013). 'Narrative identity', *Current Directions in Psychological Science*, 22(3), pp. 233–8.

2 BBC, *What's New* (2020). 'Why does Kenya produce so many top athletes?', https://www.youtube.com/watch?v=0Q_EPKiuPi8 &ab_channel=BBCWhat%E2%80%99sNew%2FActuJeunes

3 Zajonc, R.B. (1968). 'Attitudinal effects of mere exposure', *Journal of Personality and Social Psychology*, 9(2, Pt. 2), pp. 1–27.

4 From the Netflix documentary, *McGregor Forever* (2023).

5 Litovsky, Y., Loewenstein, G., Horn, S. and Olivola, C.Y. (2022). 'Loss aversion, the endowment effect, and gain-loss framing shape preferences for non-instrumental information', *Proc Natl Acad Sci U S A.*, 119(34): e2202700119. doi: 10.1073/pnas.2202700119. Epub 16 August 2022. PMID: 35972966; PMCID: PMC9407664.

6 Magness, S. (2022). *Do Hard Things*, HarperCollins, London.

7 Walter, D. (2020) *The Power of Discipline*, independently published.

8 Hare and Camerer (2009). 'The Stanford Marshmallow Experiment, 1972'. https://en.wikipedia.org/wiki/Stanford_marshmallow_experiment

9 Walter, *The Power of Discipline*.

CHAPTER 5 PHASE TWO: THE ANTI-CLIMAX OF SUCCESS

1 'Managing high achievers', https://www.mindtools.com/af7xynw/managing-high-achievers

2 Timmins, *Becoming the 0.1%*.

3 Disclaimer: cultural norms and attitudes have since changed in the Royal Marines and, as a consequence, the initiation process has been rooted out.

4 'Managing high achievers'.

CHAPTER 6 PHASE THREE: REMOVING THE STIMULUS

1 'A new life without boxing', *At Home with the Furys*, Netflix, 2023.

2 Kübler-Ross, E. (1970). *On Death and Dying*, Collier Books/ Macmillan, London.

3 Maslow, A.H. (1970). *Motivation and Personality* (2nd ed.), Harper & Row, New York.

CHAPTER 7 PHASE FOUR: MAINTAINING BEHAVIOURAL ALIGNMENT

1 Zlatopolsky, A. (2023). 'Sorry, night owls: The sleep you're missing before midnight is crucial – here's why', https://www.realsimple.com/health/preventative-health/sleep/sleep-before-midnight

2 Ibid.

3 Ibid.

4 Cleveland Clinic (2023). 'Endorphins', https://my.clevelandclinic.org/health/body/23040-endorphins#:~:text=What%20are%20endorphins%3F,your%20sense%20of%20well%2Dbeing

5 OASH (2023). 'Manage stress', https://health.gov/myhealthfinder/health-conditions/heart-health/manage-stress

6 *Becoming the 0.1%.*

7 *McGregor Forever*, Netflix.

8 Hubermanlab, https://www.instagram.com/tv/CY9PA1ehWsz/?igshid=ODhhZWM5NmIwOQ%3D%3D

9 Janssen, A. (2023). 'Irrational elite performers can teach us something about life and leadership. And it's not what you think …', https://www.linkedin.com/pulse/irrational-elite-performers-can-teach-us-something-life-janssen-1e

10 Ibid.

CHAPTER 8 PHASE FIVE: THE RESILIENCE PARADOX

1 Magness, *Do Hard Things.*

2 Ibid.

3 Ibid.

4 Nickerson, C. (2023). 'Schema theory in psychology', https://www.simplypsychology.org/what-is-a-schema.html

5 Lazard, L. (2015). *Investigating Psychology 2: From social to cognitive*, Open University, Milton Keynes.

CHAPTER 9 PHASE SIX: COGNITIVE EXHAUSTION

1 Thau, L., Gandhi, J. and Sharma, S. (2023). 'Physiology, cortisol.' In: StatPearls [internet]. Treasure Island (FL):

StatPearls Publishing, https://www.ncbi.nlm.nih.gov/books/NBK538239/

2 Ibid.

3 Mayo Clinic (2023). 'Chronic stress puts your health at risk: Chronic stress can wreak havoc on your mind and body. Take steps to control your stress', https://www.mayoclinic.org/healthy-lifestyle/stress-management/in-depth/stress/art-20046037

4 Ibid.

5 Thau et al., 2022.

6 Mayo Clinic.

7 Magness.

8 Ibid.

9 Ibid.

10 https://biomedicalodyssey.blogs.hopkinsmedicine.org/2024/01/beyond-the-renaissance-nobel-laureates-and-their-creative-pursuits/#

CHAPTER 10 PHASE SEVEN: PREVENTING BURNOUT

1 Koutsimani, P., Montgomery, A. and Georganta, K. (2019) 'The relationship between burnout, depression, and anxiety: A systematic review and meta-analysis', *Front Psychol.*, 13 Mar; 10:284. doi: 10.3389/fpsyg.2019.00284. PMID: 30918490; PMCID: PMC6424886.

2 Ibid.

3 Mack, A. (2003). 'Inattentional blindness: Looking without seeing', *Current Directions in Psychological Science*, 12(5), pp. 180–4, https://doi.org/10.1111/1467 8721.01256

4 Nixdorf, I., Beckmann, J. and Nixdorf, R. (2020). 'Psychological predictors for depression and burnout among German junior elite athletes', *Front Psychol*, 11:601. doi:10.3389/fpsyg. 2020.00601

5 Ulrich, R.S. (1981). 'Natural versus urban scenes: Some psychophysiological effects', *Environment and Behavior*, 13(5), pp. 523–56, https://doi.org/10.1177/0013916581135001

6 Falk, J.H. and Balling, J.D. (2010). 'Evolutionary influence on human landscape preference', *Environment and Behavior*, 42(4), pp. 479–93.

7 Joye, Y. and Van den Berg, A. (2011). 'Is love for green in our genes? A critical analysis of evolutionary assumptions in restorative environments research', Urban Forestry & Urban Greening, 10(4), pp. 261–8.

8 Bossomaier, T. (2012). *Introduction to the Senses: From biology to computer science*, Cambridge University Press.

9 Stevenson, M.P., Schilhab, T. and Bentsen, P. (2018). 'Attention Restoration Theory II: A systematic review to clarify attention processes affected by exposure to natural environments', *Journal of Toxicology and Environmental Health*, Part B, 21:4, pp. 227–68. doi: 10.1080/10937404.2018.1505571.

10 Hartig, T., Evans, G.W., Jamner, L.D., Davis, D.S. and Garling, T. (2003). 'Tracking restoration in natural and urban field settings', *Journal of Environmental Psychology*, 23, pp. 109–23.

11 Kaplan, S. (1995). 'The restorative benefits of nature: Toward an integrative framework', *Journal of Environmental Psychology*,

15(3), pp. 169–82, https://www.sciencedirect.com/science/article/abs/pii/0272494495900012

12 Ulrich, R.S., 1981.

13 Berto, R. (2005). 'Exposure to restorative environments helps restore attentional capacity,' *Journal of Environmental Psychology*, 25(3), pp. 249–59.

14 Hartig et al., 2003.

15 Bringslimark, T., Hartig, T. and Patil, G. (2007). 'Psychological benefits of indoor plants in workplaces: Putting experimental results into context', *HortScience*: a publication of the American Society for Horticultural Science, 42: 10.21273/HORTSCI.42.3.581.

CHAPTER 11 MENTAL HEALTH AND SUCCESS

1 Alexander Volkanovski, Emotional UFC 294 Post Fight Press Conference, https://www.youtube.com/watch?v=O23Ggl7KMQs.

2 Valcour, M. (2016). 'Beating burnout', https://hbr.org/2016/11/beating-burnout

3 Kaplan, S., 1995.

About the Author

Gareth Timmins is a former Royal Marines Commando, an empowering mindset coach and elite performance facilitator. He is the author of *Becoming the 0.1%: Thirty-four Lessons from the Diary of a Royal Marines Commando Recruit* and the founder of Nought Point One, an emerging fitness clothing brand and performance hub, focusing on high intensity physical training and extreme sports, inspired by the operational requirements of the Royal Marines.

Drawing on the life lessons learned from his Commando training and his subsequent experiences of military and private security service in the Middle East, Gareth is an accomplished motivational speaker. His journey as a Royal Marine and as a behavioural psychologist has not only shaped his character, but has also provided a unique perspective on leadership, resilience and the power of the human spirit.